The Demise of the Neandertals

Robert Sandslett

The Demise of the Neandertals

A Study on Neandertal Extinction

VDM Verlag Dr. Müller

Imprint

Bibliographic information by the German National Library: The German National Library lists this publication at the German National Bibliography; detailed bibliographic information is available on the Internet at http://dnb.d-nb.de.

Any brand names and product names mentioned in this book are subject to trademark, brand or patent protection and are trademarks or registered trademarks of their respective holders. The use of brand names, product names, common names, trade names, product descriptions etc. even without a particular marking in this works is in no way to be construed to mean that such names may be regarded as unrestricted in respect of trademark and brand protection legislation and could thus be used by anyone.

Cover image: www.purestockx.com

Publisher:
VDM Verlag Dr. Müller Aktiengesellschaft & Co. KG, Dudweiler Landstr. 125 a, 66123 Saarbrücken, Germany,
Phone +49 681 9100-698, Fax +49 681 9100-988,
Email: info@vdm-verlag.de

Copyright © 2008 VDM Verlag Dr. Müller Aktiengesellschaft & Co. KG and licensors
All rights reserved. Saarbrücken 2008

Produced in USA and UK by:
Lightning Source Inc., La Vergne, Tennessee, USA
Lightning Source UK Ltd., Milton Keynes, UK
BookSurge LLC, 5341 Dorchester Road, Suite 16, North Charleston, SC 29418, USA

ISBN: 978-3-639-06606-7

Acknowledgements

Først vil jeg takke Randi Håland og Christopher Henshilwood for deres uvurderlige kritikk og kommentarer. Uten deres hjelp hadde ikke denne boken vært til. Så vil jeg takke min samboer, Helene Simonsen. Takk for at du har holdt ut med meg gjennom det siste året, alle de sene kveldene, alt rotet og ikke minst mitt uinteressante mas om Neandertalere til alle døgnets tider. Det er lett å glemme at alle ikke er like interessert i Neandertalere som meg. Du har gjort arbeidet med denne oppgaven mye lettere enn det kunne vært. Det er jeg veldig takknemlig for. Nå er det min tur.

Table of Contents

Acknowledgements	II
Table of Contents	III
List of Figures	V

Chapter 1: Introduction 1
    Neandertal Origins 4

Chapter 2: A History of Neandertal discoveries 6
    From natural beast to cultural being 11
    Population and multiregionalism 12
    The dominating Three 13
    Culture as an ecological niche 14
    The present day situation 15

Chapter 3: Theoretical and methodological approaches to the study of Neandertal extinction 18
    Dating methods 18
    DNA analysis 20
    Material culture and human behaviour 20
    The use of negative evidence 22
    "Modern human behaviour" 23
    Neandertal/H. sapiens 25
    "Culture" or "Technocomplex" 27

Chaoter 4: The environmental background during OIS 5-3 in the Eurasian areas. 29
    Oxygen Isotope Stages 30
    The last interglacial 31
    Early glacial period 32
    Oxygen isotope stage 4 32
    Oxygen isotope stage 3 33
    Heinrich events 34
    Pollen rich marine cores 37
    Vegetational development in the Iberian Peninsula during OIS-3 38
    Neandertal occupation patterns in Eurasia during OIS-3 39

Chapter 5: Interbreeding, continuity or total replacement? 40
    The Recent African Origins Model 40
    The Hybridization and Replacement Model 41
    Multiregional evolution 41
    The Assimilation Model 42
    The fossil evidence 42
    DNA analysis 46

Chapter 6: Neandertal extinction as a result of competitive disadvantage? 50
    Fossil evidence 51
    Early Upper Palaeolithic H. sapiens 51
    Neandertal occupation across Europe during the time of transition 53
    Interaction 54
    Competition 55
    Technology 55
    Transitional industries 56
    The Aurignacian and transitional technocomplexes compared 58
    Acculturation or innovation 59
    Chronology 61
    Conclusion 63

Chapter 7: Climatic conditions as a source for extinction? 66
    Opposing hypotheses 66
    Cold or warm adapted? 71

Chapter 8: Conclusion 73
    Neandertal contradiction during the Middle- to Upper Paleolithic transition 74
    What caused the demise of the Neandertals? 76

References 78

List of Figures

Frontpage: "Old Man" of Chapelle-aux-Saints I
Frontpage: Carleton Coon's reconstruction of the "Old Man" (Coon, 1939) I

Fig. 1.1. Illustration of two main evolutionary models 4
Fig. 1.2. Map showing main Neandertal sites 5

Fig. 2.1. Neandertal 1, type specimen 6
Fig. 2.2. Marcellin Boule's reconstruction of the Chapelle-aux-Saints "Old Man" ... 9
Fig. 2.3. Fontèchevade 2 skullcap 13
Fig. 2.4. List of the most central Neandertal fossil discoveries 17

Fig. 3.1. Trait list of "modern behaviour" 24

Fig. 4.1. Comparison of the SPECMAP and GRIP 33
Fig. 4.2. Paleoclimatic reconstruction of Europe during Hengelo Interstadial 35
Fig. 4.3. Paleoclimatic reconstruction of Europe during OIS-3 cold period 36
Fig. 4.4. Climatic conditions in Iberian Peninsula based on pollen rich deep sea cores ... 37

Fig. 5.1. Four main competing models 41
Fig. 5.2. Clark Howell's illustration of Neandertal evolution 43

Fig. 6.1. Correlation between morphology and culture 56
Fig. 6.2. Distribution map of the transitional industries 57

Fig. 7.1. Geographical impact of the Campanian Ignimbrite eruption 71

Fig. 8.1. Contraction of Neandertals during Middle- to Upper Paleolithic transition ... 74
Fig. 8.2. The spread of H. sapiens across Europe during Middle- to Upper Paleolithic transition ... 75

Chapter 1
Introduction

"Homo neanderthalensis" is the species term of a morphologically distinct hominid population living in Eurasian areas from about 500,000-160,000 (depending on morphological definition) (Delson & Harvati, 2006), until approximately 30,000 years ago. During this period they managed to survive rigorous climatic deteriorations (Grip Members, 1993), forcing them into southern refugia, while successfully spreading north during subsequent climatic ameliorations (Finlayson, 2004). Although more than 100 years have passed since Neandertals were recognised as a morphologically distinct hominid group, the questions of how they lived and why they disappeared are still mostly unanswered. Their disappearance broadly coincides with the spread of anatomically modern humans across Eurasia. While some interpret this migration as the direct cause for Neandertal extinction, others view these two processes as independent of each other, thus connecting the demise of Neandertals to other factors. Anatomically modern humans (*Homo sapiens sapiens*) will be referred to as "H. sapiens" in this book.

During the course of this book the demise of the Neandertals will be reviewed from several different perspectives. By incorporating different categories of empirical data (fossil remains, genetic material, archaeological material, and paleoclimatic reconstructions), I will review where the research on the demise of Neandertals stand today, and which challenges that needs to be solved in order to progress from here. Three main questions will be central in this book:

1. Did Neanderthals and H. sapiens interbreed? And if so, to what extent, and what information can this give us on the nature of Neandertal extinction?
2. How behaviourally different were the Neanderthals from their anatomically modern contemporaries and to what extent can these differences be attributed to different biologically driven cognitive capabilities? And did these proposed behavioural differences contribute to the demise of Neandertals?
3. Can climatic, and by extension ecological conditions have influenced the demographic changes associated with the Middle- to Upper Paleolithic transition?

In chapter 2, I will present a general overview of the Neandertal research as it progressed from the first discovery in 1856 until today. This will not only provide an understanding of how the researched developed, but it will also contextualise the different views of Neandertal extinction today. By putting the present day hypotheses in an historical context, further understanding of what these hypotheses are fundamentally built upon can be obtained. It will also make visible the parallel development of both Neandertal research and human evolutionary theories in general, and how they affected, and still affect each other.

In chapter 3, the theoretical and methodological approached applied in the process of writing this book will be presented. The current practical problems when conducting both genetic analysis and radiometric dating has a significant influence on research on the demise of Neandertals. Uncertainties related to these empirical categories, and the recent progresses made will therefore be central in this chapter. Furthermore, through critique of the theoretical approaches and assumptions which have dominated this field during the past decades, I will seek to clarify why the rise and fall of Neandertals are practically as mysterious today as it was 100 years ago, and how future research on this theme can be conducted in order to progress.

In chapter 4, a general presentation of the paleoclimatic framework during the past 130,000 years will be reviewed. Climatic, and by extension ecological conditions would inevitably have large implication for the lives of Neandertals and the anatomically modern contemporaries. The reconstruction of the paleoclimatic conditions in the Neandertal world will be used as a background from which an increased understanding of the empirical data presented in the subsequent chapters can be obtained.

In chapter 5, the Neandertal extinction will be discussed with emphasis on the fossil record. Fossil remains are crucial in connecting cultural attributes to Neandertals and H. sapiens. They can also be very useful in providing direct dates of Neandertal occupation, as well as contributing to establish a connection between species and cultural attributes. Further information on the extinction of Neandertals may also be sought through the extraction of genetic material from both Neandertal and H. sapiens DNA. If Neandertals and H. sapiens interbred, even on a small scale, this would give valuable information on Neandertals as a species, but also on the nature of the proposed contact between Neandertals and H. sapiens.

In chapter 6, the Middle- to Upper Paleolithic transition will be reviewed with emphasis on the archaeological record. The fossil record from this period is scarce. In order to create a hypothesis regarding the extinction of Neandertals, archaeological material must therefore play a crucial role. This period represents one of the most distinct in human prehistory. The archaeological record reveals major changes during a relatively short time period. Behavioural aspect of the Middle- to Upper Paleolithic transition is central for understanding the complexity of the many processes involved in the extinction of an entire hominid population. Did Neandertals become extinct as a result of not being able to adapt (behaviourally and cognitively) to the environmental and cultural changes manifested in the Middle- to Upper Paleolithic transition? As will be shown in chapter 5, the value of DNA analyses trying to examine the question of interbreeding, is greatly dependant upon reconstructions of how, and to what extent Neandertals and H. sapiens interacted.

In order to create a coherent hypothesis of the processes involved in Neandertal extinction, general assumption between "race" and "culture" has to be made (Straus, 2005). Due to few fossil remains being recovered, relative to the abundant archaeological material, generalised affiliations between taxonomic entities like "Neandertals" and "Mousterian" is unavoidable. Notwithstanding, it has to be explicitly stated that there is no theoretical or empirical foundation for developing strictly species-specific behavioural hypotheses (e.g. Klein, 1999b).

In chapter 7, the possible correlation between the cultural and demographic changes and the climatic oscillations recorded during the Middle- to Upper Paleolithic will be scrutinised. The new and improved paleoclimatic reconstructions provided by examinations of Greenland ice cores (e.g. Bond *et al*, 1993, Dansgaard *et al*, 1993, GRIP Members, 1993) and pollen rich deep sea cores (Sánchez Goñi *et al*, 1999, 2000, 2002), shows that the climatic conditions during the spread of H. sapiens across Eurasia and the subsequent demise of Neandertal was far more oscillatory than previously assumed. How did these climatic conditions affect the human populations living in these areas during this period, and can climatic conditions be directly correlated to the extinction of the Neandertals?

In the concluding chapter, I will review what information this book has provided on the extinction of the Neandertals. Is it possible to correlate the different empirical categories reviewed in this work in order to create a holistic hypothesis? And if so, what caused the demise of the Neandertals?

Neandertal origins

The origin of the Neandertals is a matter of continued controversy. The relationship between Neandertals and H. sapiens can be organised into two dichotomised views. The differences between them can be regarded as due to having fundamentally different views on how the evolutionary process in general should be explained. There is currently a general consensus that Neandertals evolved in Europe during the Middle Pleistocene (ca. 780,000 - 130,000 years ago), from local *Homo erectus* populations, or an intermediate species (*Homo heidelbergensis* or "archaic" *Homo sapiens*) (Stringer & Gamble, 1993).

Population replacement
Proponents of population replacement, postulate a relatively recent origin of anatomically modern humans within the African continent (Stringer et al, 1984). By emphasising morphological (Klein, 1999a) and genetic (Krings et al, 1997) differences between Neandertals and H. sapiens, they argue that Neandertals should be regarded as a separate species, *Homo neanderthalensis*. After *Homo erectus* first migrated out of Africa about 1 million years ago (Stringer et al, 1984), they propose that Neandertals and H. sapiens evolved separately into distinct species in Eurasia and Africa, respectively. Thus, Neandertals would have accumulated their distinct morphological features through natural selection of cold adapted features and physical strength (Stringer, 1992).

Regional continuity
Multiregional evolutionists emphasise population continuity through gene flow. After the initial dispersal of *Homo erectus* across the world, separated populations would develop distinctive morphological features through local adaptation. However, contrary to proponents of population replacement, they advocate an evolutionary continuity due to the different hominid populations not being isolated enough to develop into separated species (e.g. Wolpoff, 1989, 1992, Frayer et al, 1993, Wolpoff et al, 2004). They therefore regard all hominid populations subsequent to the dispersal of *Homo erectus* as members of the same species, *Homo sapiens*, thus arguing that the morphological differences seen between Neandertals and anatomically moderns are on a subspecies level (Relethford, 2001).

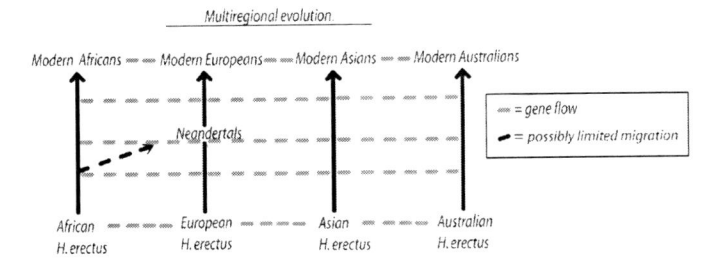

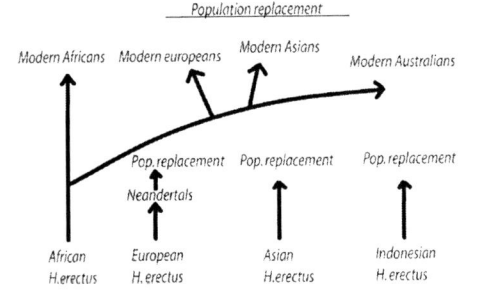

(**Fig. 1.1.** Modified after: Stringer, 1992a)

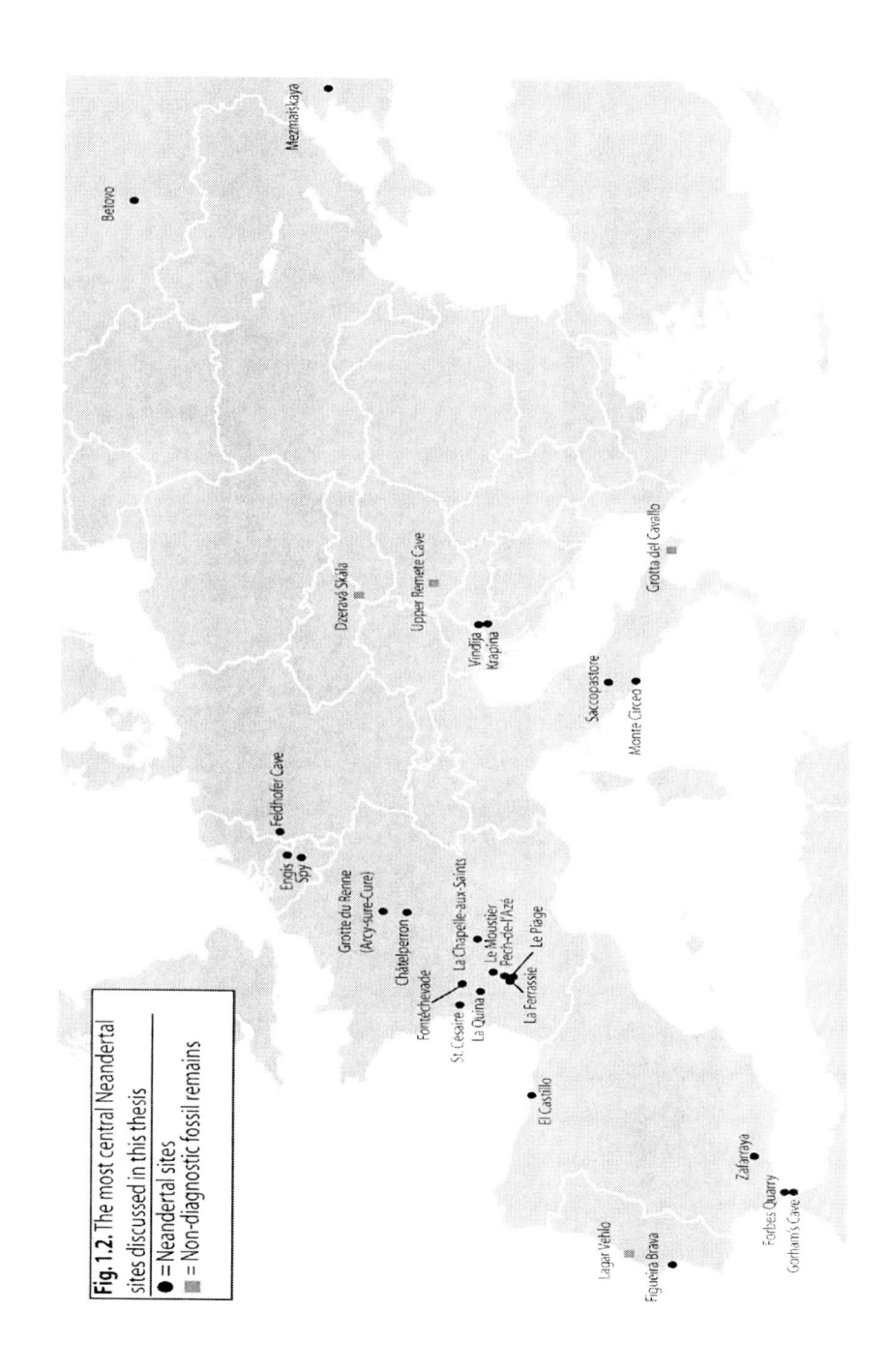

Fig. 1.2. The most central Neandertal sites discussed in this thesis
● = Neandertal sites
■ = Non-diagnostic fossil remains

Chapter 2

A history of Neandertal discoveries

In 1856, at Feldhofer Cave in Neander Tal (Valley, originally spelled "Thal" in German) in Germany, workers found a partial skeleton that they believed belonged to a cave bear. Still the foreman decided that the largest bones were to be set aside and handed over to a local schoolteacher named Johann Karl Fuhlrott for educational purposes. Fuhlrott recognized that these skeletal remains were in fact not from a cave bear, but from a human with morphological features very different from modern humans (fig. 2.1). He therefore sought professional help from biologist Hermann Schaafhausen at the University of Bonn. Through anatomical analysis, Schaafhausen concluded that the remains represented a descendant of the "primitive races" initially believed to inhabit North-western Europe (Trinkhaus & Shipman, 1992).

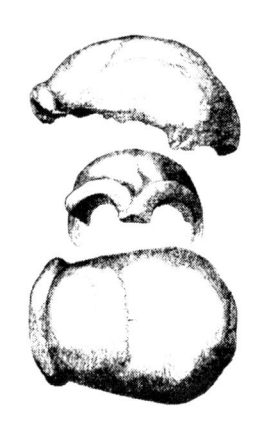

Fig. 2.1. Neandertal 1, type specimen. Found in Feldhofer Cave, 1856 (Huxley, 1863).

When Schaafhausen presented his examination of the Feldhofer remains later that year, he strongly argued that the unique morphological features displayed in the skeleton were non-pathological and that the remains represented a normal individual of a new human species (Howells, 1960). His view was strongly opposed by many of his contemporary science colleagues. Perhaps the most important scholar to argue against Schaafhausen was Rudolf Virchow from the University of Berlin (Trinkhaus & Shipman, 1992). Today, Virchow is regarded as the founder of modern pathology, and he strongly rejected evolutionary ideas throughout his career (Trinkhaus & Shipman, 1992). The skeletal remains from the Feldhofer Cave, Virchow believed to be the remains of a person who suffered from the pathological disease "rickets" and possibly antemortem blows to the head (Klein, 1999a). Based on his interpretation of the fossil being an older man when he died, Virchow also concluded that he could only reach such an age by living a recent sedentary agrarian lifestyle, thus not originating from an ancient hunter-gatherer society (Brace, 1964).

During the time of the initial Feldhofer Cave discovery, science was a highly hierarchical and centralized discipline. Virchow's view was therefore strengthened by his dominant place in German scientific communities. One of the major problems in initial Neandertal research was that evolutionary theories were far from generally accepted during the time when the original Neandertal was first discovered (Brace, 1964). Although Charles Darwin published *The Origin of Species* in 1859, he did not mention the Neandertals in his theory of evolution. One of Darwin's first followers, Thomas Henry Huxley, was probably the first scholar to explore Neandertals significance in human evolution (Huxley, 1863). In his series of essays called *Evidence as to Man's Place in Nature*, published in 1863, he concluded that "though truly the most pithecoid of known human skulls, the Neanderthal cranium is by no means so isolated as it appears to be at first, but forms, in reality, the extreme term of a series leading gradually from it to the highest and best developed of human crania (Huxley, 1863:13f).

William King, an Irish anatomist, published a paper in January 1864 where he argued that the finds from Feldhofer Cave should be classified as a new species of humans, *Homo neanderthalensis*. In 1904, the German word for Valley, "Thal" was changed to "Tal", and nearly 50 years later, in 1952 Henri Vallois proposed that the spelling of Neandertal should match the German language. Therefore, "Neandertal" is the most common spelling, except for England where "Neanderthal" is still widely used (Trinkhaus & Shipman, 1992).

Later in 1864 Hugh Falconer, a British palaeontologist, classified a skull from Forbe's Quarry in Gibraltar, found in 1848, as a Neandertal. His classification raised only minor interest among his colleagues, as did George Busk's and Paul Boca's similar conclusions in 1865 and 1869, respectively. The Neandertal remains from Gibraltar were not to be thoroughly examined, and subsequently accepted as Neandertal until 1908, by William Sollas (Sollas, 1908). Even earlier, in 1830, Phillipe-Charles Schmerling, found three cranial remains associated with extinct animals (Trinkhaus & Shipman, 1992). One of these three craniums was classified as Neandertal by Charles Fraipont in 1936 (Klein, 1999a).

Rudolf Virchow's pathological view remained dominant, especially in his own country Germany, until 1886 when the two Belgians Marcel de Puydt and Marie Joseph Maximin found two almost completely intact skeletons at Spy d'Orneau, Belgium (Trinkhaus & Shipman, 1992). These two skeletons closely resembled the original Neandertal skull from Feldhofer. Having three almost complete skeletons, which showed almost identical distinctive anatomical deviation from that of modern humans, made it utterly unlikely that all three had the exact same pathological history.

In 1906, a Croatian palaeontologist, Karl Gorjanović-Kramberger published a paper called *Der Diluviale Mensch von Krapina in Kroatien*. This paper was based on his excavations at Krapina, Croatia in the years 1899-1905 (Russell, 1987). His excavation produced almost a thousand human bone fragments originating from somewhere between two and three dozen individuals, three thousand bones from animals and also thousands of stone tools and flakes. Gorjanović-Kramberger concluded that the stone tools were of the Mousterian type classified by Gabriel De Mortillet some twenty years earlier. The human skeletal remains featured the same "primitive" characteristics as the Neandertal finds from 1856. Following up on numerous preceding claims, Gorjanović-Kramberger also argued that the Krapina Neandertals were cannibals. He noted that the skeletal remains were scattered seemingly unsystematically around the site. They were also highly fragmented, and he found evidence of some bones being exposed to fire and that all of the largest bones were exploited for marrow. Later on it was argued that the claim for an unusually high degree of breakage in the Krapina remains may not be attributed to cannibalism, but rather to excavation methods and sedimentary pressure and/or roof falls (Russell, 1987).

The large amount of Neandertal remains recovered at Krapina doubled the total amount of individuals discovered (Trinkhaus & Shipman, 1992). Now there were about seventy individuals in total, confirming that Neandertals were not, as Virchow had argued, simply pathological humans. Still, the question of Neandertals place in human evolution was far from answered. Gorjanović-Kramberger felt that the Krapina Neandertals and their exclusive association with Mousterian tools demonstrated that they were the direct ancestors to modern humans. Hermann Klaatsch, a German anthropologist, strongly opposed Gorjanović-Kramberger's view. He argued that among the Krapina remains were also anatomically modern humans, which he called *Homo aurignacensis*, implying that these two species were in fact contemporary (Klaatsch, 1924).

In 1908 Otto Hauser, a Swiss-German amateur found a complete skeleton of a Neandertal adolescent at Le Moustier, France. His find showed a clear connection between Neandertals and the Mousterian stone tool type named after the same site. Hauser's second find came from a site called Combe Capelle in the same French region as Le Moustier. He excavated a burial site of a skeleton of modern anatomy, clearly associated with so-called *Aurignacian* stone tools, named after the French site of Aurignac. The skeleton was buried only inches above the Neandertal associated Mousterian level. To Klaatsch, the brief time period separating the Neandertal and H. sapiens remains at Le Moustier made it highly unlikely that Neandertals could have evolved into sophisticated modern humans. Klaatsch used these finds to further his argument, claiming that the different human species today evolved from different ancient species, namely the Negroid race that originated from Neandertals, and Caucasians that originated from the makers of the advanced Aurignacian stone tools, *Homo aurignacensis* (Klaatsch, 1924).

In 1909, Denis Peyrony and Louis Capitan found an adult male Neandertal skeleton at La Ferrassie. The year after, they found another Neandertal fossil, this time an adult female. Another French site, called La Quina was excavated by Henri Martin in 1910 and revealed bones from two more Neandertal individuals.

In 1908 two French brothers, Amèdèe and Jean Bouyssonie excavated a small cave in La Chapelle-aux-Saints, France. They found a skeleton that was until then the best preserved find, and which was to become the best known Neandertal ever discovered, the so-called "Old Man". The skeleton was handed over to the French palaeontologist Marcellin Boule who, perhaps not so coincidently, shared the excavators view on Neandertals place in human evolution. Therefore, the result of Boule's examination of the skeleton was not surprising. Boule classified the La Chapelle-aux-Saints Neandertal as a separate species, *Homo neanderthalensis*. Giving it such a name emphasized that Neandertals did not have an influence on modern H. sapiens, but that Neandertals were in fact an evolutionary dead end (Hammond, 1982). His work strongly emphasized differences between anatomically modern humans and Neandertals and not similarities. Detailed descriptions of each part of the skeleton were used to illustrate that Neandertals had simian features as opposed to the elegant features of anatomically modern humans (Fig 2.2). He estimated the

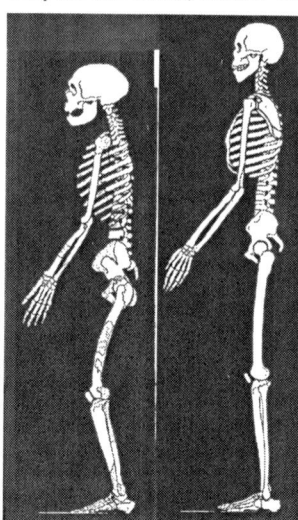

Fig. 2.2. Boule's famous depiction of the "Old Man's" posture (Boule & Vallois, 1957).

"Old Man's" age at approximately fifty years at the time of death, which more recently has been adjusted to about thirty years of age (Dawson & Trinkhaus, 1997). Although the Neandertal from La Chapelle-aux-Saints clearly had been suffering from arthritis, a broken rib and a badly injured hip, Boule disregarded these facts, presenting the Old Man as a normal and healthy Neandertal. Using the La Ferrassie remains as stand-ins where the La Chapelle-aux-Saints skeleton was badly preserved, Boule presented the Neandertal posture as especially different and simian compared to modern humans (Stringer & Gamble, 1993).

Boule's publication on the remains from La Chapelle-aux-Saints did not only have a profound and long lasting impact on the image of Neandertals; it also had a major impact on science in general. Boule's methodological work closely followed the procedures used for examining animal species, and thus established the paleontology of humans, later called paleoanthropology (Trinkhaus & Shipman, 1992). Marcellin Boule also used his results to point out that human evolution did not follow a unilineal path as Gabriel de Mortillet had argued. He argued instead that human evolution was of closer resemblance to a bush, containing different branches, whereas some were evolutionary dead ends (Boule & Vallois, 1957).

From 1920 onwards, the pace of Neandertal discoveries slowed. This was probably because the most promising sites known at the time had already been excavated and scientists were later adopting more time consuming excavation methods (Klein 1999a). In 1929, an English archaeologist named Dorothy Garrod led the excavations undertaken in two caves at Mount Carmel in Palestine, now Israel. The caves were called Mugharet et-Tabun and Mugharet es-Skhul. In addition to numerous faunal remains and stone tools, Garrod's work revealed about ten partial skeletons from the Skhul cave and a partial skeleton of a female at Tabun (Garrod & Bate, 1937). An American student called Theodore McCown and the retired Scottish anatomist called Arthur Keith carried out examinations of the remains. The skeletons from Skhul predominantly resembled anatomically modern humans, but the partial skeleton of a female from the nearby Tabun cave was different. Although she had relatively modern looking limb bones, the skull undoubtedly had a Neandertal shape, proving for the first time the presence of Neandertals outside of Europe. Perhaps most surprising was that the modern looking remains from Skhul were clearly associated with Mousterian type stone tools. If these skeletons were in fact anatomically modern, it would seem like they were not only contemporary with European Neandertals, but possibly even preceded them. However,

McCown and Keith concluded that the differences seen between the finds from Skhul and Tabun should be considered as morphological variation of a single population of Neandertals (McCown & Keith, 1939).

From natural beast to cultural being
Until the Second World War, racial separation and ascribing certain qualities to different racial groups was dominant in society in general, as well as in the research of human evolution. In trying to outdistance oneself from the defeated Nazis, racial issues became controversial after the war. This led many scholars not only to emphasize the similarities between Neandertals and anatomically modern humans but also to fuse them into the same hominid species, *Homo sapiens* (Trinkhaus & Shipman, 1992).

Ever since the early days of the 20th century it was considered a known fact that Neandertals buried their dead. Otto Hauser was the first to pronounce that he had found evidence of a Neandertal burial at Le Moustier in 1909 (Trinkhaus & Shipman, 1992). Further evidence accumulated from sites like La Chapelle-aux-Saints, La Ferrassie and many other sites. At the time, burial of the dead was not in itself seen as reflecting symbolic behaviour. Evidence of Neandertal symbolic behaviour from Monte Circeo in Italy therefore came as a great surprise to the scientific communities. Workers accidentally found an unknown cave, dubbed Grotta Guattari, within which they discovered a Neandertal skull situated face down on the cave floor. According to an amateur fossil hunter named Alberto Blanc, the Neandertals skull had been separated from its body post mortem and were situated within an arranged circle of stones, thus indicating a complex symbolic and possibly religious expression. More recent studies from Grotta Guattari questions the circumstances under which the original study was undertaken, concluding that the cave was probably predominantly a "hyaena-den" and that the symbolic context attributed to the position of the skull was most likely misinterpreted (Stiner 1991:117).

In addition to the Monte Circeo finds, accumulating evidence of fossil remains of hominids that appeared to be even more simian-like than Neandertals was found around the world. Today these fossils are classified as for example *Homo erectus* and *Australopithecus*. Compared to these "primitive" and "ape-like" creatures the Neandertals seemed all the more closely related to modern day humans (Trinkhaus & Shipman, 1992).

Population and multiregionalism

Neandertal research was until the 1920's predominately limited to morphological studies of fossils and discussion regarding evolution in general. Little effort had been made on creating an explanatory model where regional differences, ecological factors, climatic influence and geographical isolation were taken into consideration. Aleš Hrdlička, an American anthropologist, was one of the first to explore the importance of local environmental conditions in the physical evolution of humans (e.g. Hrdlička, 1926, 1927). Hrdlička was a strong supporter of the view that Neandertals were the direct ancestors of anatomically modern humans. He therefore connected the characteristic robust features of the Neandertals to their association with the harsh environments of glacial Europe (Hrdlička, 1926). A German anatomist, Franz Weidenreich, further developed Hrdlička's hypothesis from eurocentric to multiregional. Weidenreich suggested a scenario where different modern populations of the world were descendants of different fossil species due to regional isolation, although proposing some degree of inter-population gene flow (Weidenreich, 1947).

However, Clark Howell's multiregional hypothesis was to be the most influential. The American anthropologist published his master thesis on Neandertals in 1951. Howell emphasized regional differences, and his study of Neandertal fossils led him to divide them into two main groups. He noticed that the features which were regarded as strictly Neandertal, in his view their robust build and large-brows, seemed to be restricted to the Last Glacial in Europe. On the other hand, Neandertals associated with older, interglacial layers were more widespread geographically and could be characterized as more modern looking than the glacial Neandertals or *Classic Neandertals* as they were dubbed by him. Therefore, Howell concluded that the European record was characterized by a "Neandertalization" through time (Howell 1957). The mechanisms behind the development could, according to Howell be attributed to two factors; adaptation to the harsh glacial environment and/or genetic drift. Genetic drift was a rather new concept when Howell presented his work. It was based on the notion that certain individuals within a single population might be more successful in mating than others. When repeated over several generations these individuals genetic features may become dominant (Lewin & Foley, 2004, Mayr, 2001).

Clark Howell proposed that Neandertals that were not associated with glacial Europe, like the remains from Mount Carmel and Krapina, did not evolve into classic Neandertals but underwent what he called a "sapiensation", evolving into modern looking Aurignacian tool makers. He then described a scenario of increasingly benign climate in the middle of the Last Glaciation conditioned the spread of anatomically modern humans across Europe.

The dominating Three

In 1958, a former student of Marcellin Boule, named Henri Vallois, published an influential paper where he stated that the study of human evolution was dominated by three main hypotheses, named Presapiens, Preneandertal and Neandertal (Trinkhaus & Shipman, 1992).

"The Presapiens hypothesis" was based on the Neandertals not being predecessors of anatomically modern humans. Marcellin Boule's famous examination of the La Chapelle-aux-Saints Neandertal had shown that they were very primitive and simian-like, and could therefore not be a close relative to modern humans. Instead, proponents of the Presapiens hypothesis (e.g. Keith, 1927, Vallois, 1949, Boule & Vallois, 1957) suggested that large-brained modern humans were so distinct that they must have had a long individual evolutionary history. Without having supporting evidence available they suggested that instead of evolving from Neandertals, modern humans derived from a human race which should be tracked as far back as into the Pliocene (Keith, 1927). During this long lasting evolutionary period Neandertals represented one among many evolutionary dead ends (Trinkhaus & Shipman 1992). The Presapiens hypothesis was largely discredited by the revealing of the Piltdown fraud (Weiner *et al*, 1953) and similar discredit of supporting evidence from Moulin Quignon, Galley Hill and Ipswich (Trinkhaus & Shipman, 1992). The hypothesis was simply lacking enough substantial evidence. Still supporters of the Presapiens theory argued that the recently discovered skullcaps from Fontèchevade provided the crucial proof of modern humans evolving from a Presapiens race. According to Vallois the skullcaps were characterized by their lack of heavy brow-ridges in spite of being undoubtedly ancient (Vallois, 1954). However, such an interpretation relies on a considerable reconstruction of the skullcaps because they were highly fragmented (Fig. 2.3).

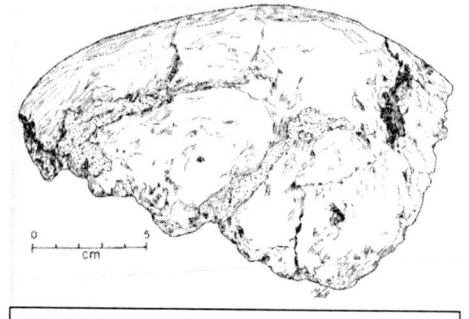

Fig. 2.3. Fontèchevade 2 skullcap.

13

"The Preneandertal hypothesis" was formed and articulated perhaps most clearly by Sergio Sergi (e.g. 1948a,b). The Italian palaeontologist argued that a less specialised type of humans existed in Europe before the Neandertals. His view coincided with Clark Howells division between the oldest Neandertal fossils and the classic Neandertals. The oldest Neandertals, or pre-Neandertals as they were dubbed by Sergi, seemed not to have developed the extreme anatomy which was regarded as typical Neandertal. He therefore argued that both modern humans and Neandertals had developed from these pre-Neandertals.

"The Neandertal hypothesis", as it was dubbed by Vallois, was based on the Neandertals being the direct ancestors of modern humans. Among the chief advocates of this hypothesis was Aleš Hrdlička, who firmly believed that Neandertals merely represented a phase in the evolution of humans (1927). Hrdlička also argued that this development was clearly represented in the stone tool technologies associated with Neandertals and anatomically modern humans. The Aurignacian culture was argued to be a direct outgrowth of the Mousterian. Although Vallois placed Weidenreich within this hypothesis, this was arguably somewhat inaccurate (Trinkhaus & Shipman, 1992). Weidenreich also believed that Neandertals had evolved directly into modern humans, he saw the Neandertals as being confined to Europe, and that other species in other parts of the world also evolved into modern humans, explaining the presence of different human species in the modern day world. Weidenreich originally attempted to visually present his theory by making a criss-cross diagram illustrating different geographical populations evolving through time (Trinkhaus & Shipman, 1992). His diagram was arguably difficult to interpret and therefore his theories did not become fully recognised until the English anthropologist William Howells published his simplification of Weidenreich's theory of geographical variation in his textbook called *Mankind in the Making* in 1960 (Howells, 1960). Carleton Coon, an American physical anthropologist also presented a simplified illustration of Weidenreich's diagram, but he emphasised the importance of total population isolation through a long time period (Coon, 1962). Weidenreich on the other hand suggested a continued genetic connection between populations from different geographical regions.

Culture as an ecological niche
During the 1960's, an increasing emphasis on culture as a driving force for human evolution started to dominate the research. Perhaps most famous is the classic book by Lee and DeVore,

Man the Hunter, proclaiming that hunting strategies was the main factor for the evolutionary development of human traits like bipedal walking, language, nuclear family arrangement etc. (Lee & DeVore, 1968). C. Loring Brace also promoted a scenario where culture was the main force behind human physical evolution. The use of tools instead of one's mouth had over time reduced the Neandertal prominent facial characters (which he regarded as essentially the only morphological differentiation) into modern looking humans (Brace, 1963).

Further emphasis on the cultural attributions was provided by Ralph S. Solecki. Based on his excavations at Shanidar in Iraq, Solecki excavated a Neandertal burial (Solecki, 1975), supposedly buried with flowers (Leroi-Gourhan, 1975). To Solecki, this was proof of the Neandertals being capable of human qualities like ritual behaviour. In 1979, another important discovery was to change the long persisting view of Neandertals being culturally archaic. The Neandertal skull found close to Saint-Césaire in France (Lévêque & Vandermeersch, 1980), in a Châtelperronian context came as a surprise. The Châtelperronian technocomplex, being a blade-based industry, had for long been view as exclusively made by H. sapiens (Gambier, 1989). The discovery immediately evoke debate, each researcher incorporating the new evidence into their pre-proposed scenarios (e.g. Wolpoff, 1981, Stringer *et al*, 1984).

The present day situation
Over the past two decades, the debate regarding the place of Neandertals in human prehistory has been dominated by two competing models; the Multiregional Model, and the Recent African Origins Model (RAO). Today, the Recent African Origins model dominates the field, although an increasing amount of empirical data is complicating the clear cut population replacement proposed for the Eurasian record (e.g. McBrearty & Brooks, 2000).

The RAO model, based on William Howell's "Noah's Ark model" (1976), advocates the view that intruding anatomically modern humans replaced the local Neandertals within a relatively short span of time, leading to the total extinction of Neandertals. Central to the RAO model is the idea that Neandertals became extinct with little or no gene exchange (Klein, 1999a, 2003, Mellars, 1996, Vandermeersch, 1989, Stringer, 1989). The total replacement of one population by another, without significant genetic exchange, is often explained by behavioural, and by extension competitive advantages. The Middle- to Upper Paleolithic transition is seen by proponents of the RAO model as the physical manifestation of one population being rapidly replaced by another. Therefore, they tend to emphasise the abruptness of this transition, applying terms like *"human revolution"* (Binford, 1989). Emphasising the proposed primitiveness of the Neandertal populations represented by the Middle Paleolithic Neandertals as apposed to the behaviourally "modern" H. sapiens of the Upper Paleolithic, reinforces the impression of the abrupt nature of the Middle- to Upper Paleolithic empirical record.

Proponents of the Multiregional model emphasise the importance of adaptation to regional conditions. The model is based on the work undertaken by Weidenreich (1947) and Carleton Coon (e.g. 1955, 1962). They view the Neandertals as merely a necessary stage in the human evolution from *Homo erectus* to *Homo sapiens*. On a universal scale, Neandertals are portrayed as the European version of archaic populations inhabiting the entire old world, subsequently evolving into anatomically modern *Homo sapiens*. As the earliest proponents of Multiregional Evolution did not explain why present day populations do not consist of several different human species as a consequence of independent evolution in different populations, the Multiregional model has been modified during later years. Present day multiregionalists propose some degree of gene flow across geographically distinct populations, prohibiting divergence into separate species.

Another important point to be made is that many multiregionalists by no means preclude African populations being ancestors to present day Europeans; they simply propose a scenario where the local Neandertal populations played a significant role in the development of these populations:

> *"To be clear, "significant" in this context means that Neandertal are among the ancestors of later Europeans, not that Neandertals are the unique or only ancestor of later Europeans."* (Wolpoff *et al*, 2004:528).

Due to a major expansion of the available empirical record, in addition to a plurality of theoretical and methodological approaches applied, several new models have been proposed in recent years. In addition to the diametrically opposed Multiregional and RAO models, the intermediate models called "The hybridization and replacement model" and "The assimilation model" adds on to an increasingly diversified debate (Aiello, 1993). These four competing models will be further discussed in chapter 5, 6 and 7.

Date	Place Name	Country	Researcher	Comments
1830	Engis Cave	Belgium	Schmerling	Recognised as Neandertal by Charles Fraipont in 1936 (Klein, 1999a).
1848	Forbes Quarry	Gibraltar		Recognised as Neandertal in 1908 (Sollas, 1908).
1856	Neander Thal	Germany	Fuhlrott and Schaafhausen	The first recognised Neandertal (called Neandertal 1).
1886	Spy Cave	Belgium	De Puydt & Maximin	Served as important confirmation of Neandertal 1
1906	Krapina	Croatia	Gorjanović-Kramberger	Recovered between fourteen and eighty-two individuals (Klein 1999a).
1908	Le Moustier 1	France	Hauser	Established the association between Mousterian technocomplex and Neandertals
1908	La Chapelle-aux-Saints	France	Amèdèe and Jean Bouyssonie	Called "Old Man" by Boule (Boule & Vallois, 1957)
1909-1912	La Ferrassie	France	Peyrony & Capitan	Skeletal remains used by Boule to reconstruct the "Old Man's" posture.
1911	La Quina	France	Martin	
1929	Tabun	Israel	Garrod	Results published by McCown & Keith (1939)
1930	Skhul	Israel	Garrod	Classified as Neandertal by McCown and Keith (1939). Later classified as archaic H. sapiens (Howell, 1957).
1939	Grotta Guattari	Italy	Blanc	Found in a putative symbolic context. Contextual validity later questioned (Stiner, 1991).
1953-1960	Shanidar	Iraq	Solecki	9 individuals (Shanidar 1-9) recovered. Putative flower burial (Solecki, 1975, Leroi-Gourhan, 1975).
1979	Saint-Césaire	France	Lévêque & Vandermeersch	Found in association with Châtelperronian stone tools.
1999	Abrigo do Lagar Velho	Portugal	Duarte and Zilhão	Hominid child skeleton displaying both Neandertal and H. sapiens morphology (Duarte et al, 1999).

Fig. 2.4. *List of the most central Neandertal fossil discoveries*

Chapter 3

Theoretical and methodological approaches to the study of Neandertal extinction

Archaeological research, as is the case in other sciences, is highly influenced by the theoretical, methodological and terminological approaches applied. To some extent, these factors exist *a priori*, but they will also partly be reconsidered and revised during a critical scientific working process. The first step in a scientific work should therefore always be an identification of the theoretical and methodological preconceptions applied, and a critical discussion regarding the possibilities and restrictions they represent. Furthermore, certain terms carry in them a set of preconceived assumptions. When using such terms it is important to both recognize their effect on the research undertaken, but also to recognize the cognitive action it will have on readers. This chapter will seek to present a critical review of some of the theoretical, methodological and terminological approaches applied in the process of creating this book.

Dating methods

Human prehistory is formed by a series of connected and independent processes. Radiocarbon dating only provides dates for punctuated events. In order to transform these events into the actual processes they are snapshots of, the gap between them must be connected by applying qualified assumptions (Pettitt, 1999). It is during the work of transforming punctuated events, provided by the empirical record, into meaningful processes that hypotheses (and the differences between them) are created. The more punctuated events available on a chronological timeline, the fewer gaps will have to be bridged by assumptions and interpretations.

Any scenario involving the succession of H. sapiens and subsequent demise of the Neandertals must rely on a fairly secure, high resolution chronological framework. However, creating such a chronological framework has proven difficult. While intra-site stratigraphic sequences can provide useful information on the relative chronology between Neandertals and H. sapiens, such sequences are rare and up-to-date excavations of such sequences even rarer. Furthermore, stratigraphic sequences are not satisfactory when dealing with the archaeological record on a regional level. Therefore, one is dependent upon inter-site comparisons of radiometrically dated material (Zilhão, 2006d).

^{14}C dating is the most commonly applied dating method when modelling the Middle- to Upper Paleolithic transition. Unfortunately, ^{14}C dating is far from an optimal dating method for this period. Radiocarbon dating has a total range of approximately 50 thousand years (kyr) (Hughen et al, 2004), but samples older than 23 kyr tends to produce dates which are significantly underestimated (Hopkin, 2006). These problems are due to time-varying processes which affect the ^{14}C production in the atmosphere and varying distribution of ^{14}C among active global carbon reservoirs (Hughen et al, 2004). Furthermore, the low proportion of carbon remaining in the oldest samples results in even miniscule quantities of contaminations having large implications for the obtained dates (Mellars, 2006a).

In trying to overcome these discrepancies, several calibration methods are applied. Correlation of ^{14}C and Uranium-thorium dates from corals has provided a marine calibration curve applicable for the last 30 kyr (Bard et al, 1990). A similar calibration curve has been established by the correlation between a series of marine ^{14}C measurements and the stratigraphic sequence recorded in the Greenland Ice Sheet Project 2 (GISP2) (Hughen et al, 2004). In addition to numerous other calibration studies (e.g. Voelker et al, 1998, Fairbanks et al, 2005, Chiu et al, 2005), these calibrations revealed that not only did the traditional ^{14}C dates diverge sharply from the actual calendrical years, but also that the results of the different calibration methods differed from one another (Mellars, 2006a). As shown by Kitagawa and van der Plicht (1998), the deviation between radiocarbon years and calendrical years beyond 31 kyr is not constant. Therefore, one cannot simply add 3000 years to the obtained ^{14}C dates, as has been done by several authors (Zilhão & d'Errico, 1999). Another implication of the discrepancies between different sources of calibration is that direct comparison of different dating methods, like ESR, TL, OSL, and radiocarbon dates is not secure (Van der Plicht, 1999). As for the problems of contamination, several improvements have recently been achieved. Advancement in the accelerator mass spectrometry (AMS) instrumentations has substantially improved the pretreatment techniques. By applying ultrafiltration preparation techniques the risk of contamination has been significantly reduced (Bronk Ramsey et al, 2004).

The recent advancement in several aspect of radiocarbon dating the Middle- to Upper Paleolithic transition has been dubbed by Paul Mellars a "radiocarbon revolution" (2006a). Notwithstanding, the work of creating a secure chronological framework for the transition is still connected with substantial difficulties. As will be reviewed later in this book, the current debate on the demise of the Neandertals is still highly influenced by the lack of consensus regarding the appropriate application of the obtained dating results. As different authors tend to interpret dating results differently, both the timing of the Neandertal demise and by extension, the climatic and demographic conditions associated with this event varies greatly within different hypotheses (d'Errico & Sánchez Goñi, 2003).

DNA analysis
Since the late 1980's, DNA analysis has been incorporated in the existing models regarding the demise of the Neandertals. Initially, the DNA studies showing that all modern day populations had a common ancestor on the African continent some 200,000 years ago (Cann *et al*, 1987) were seen as unequivocally supporting the population replacement hypothesis. In later years, this was supported by several studies confirming the genetic distance between Neandertals and modern humans (e.g. Krings *et al*, 1999). However, the critical voices questioning the supposed unambiguous nature of the DNA studies have recently grown stronger (Abbott, 2003). The critique is of both technical and theoretical nature, and will be further discussed in chapter 5. If these problems can be solved in the feature, DNA analysis can prove to be a crucial tool in examining the demise of the Neandertals. Analysis of both ancient DNA (aDNA) and extant DNA lineages may be helpful in examining whether or not Neandertals and H. sapiens interbred. Interaction involving interbreeding (even on such a small scale that it is not genetically important) would imply that the interaction, at least on a cultural scale, was arguably significant.

Material culture and human behaviour
The physical remains of human activity, material culture, are the main sources of information in archaeology. What is material culture and how does it relate to the actual societies and individuals that created them? During the early part of the 20th century, archaeology was dominated by a "Culture-historical" approach. The focus of this paradigm was mainly on a newly introduced term, "culture" (Olsen, 1997). The general emphasis on ethnic groups and their supposedly inherited qualities, led archaeologist to identify such ethnic group in the archaeological record and trace them back to a place of origin (Trigger, 1989). From the

beginning of the 1960's, the Cultural-historical archaeology, as it came to be known, was increasingly seen as insufficient in many aspects of exploring prehistory. One of the main objections was that its emphasis on typological arrangement made it a discipline dominated by authority. It was the strength of a scientist's authority which destined if his research was "good" or "bad" (Trinkhaus & Shipman, 1992). The "New Archaeology", or "Processual" archaeology, tried to create a system of examining material culture that could be valued independent of the scientist. Inspired by the neo-evolutionism of the 1960's, processual archaeologists saw culture as a tool for adaptation. Therefore, cultural elements will adjust according to ecological fluctuations because of a universal human tendency to develop toward equilibrium or symbiosis with its internal elements and its surroundings. Development or change is the result of cause and effect. Processual archaeology was dominated by a deterministic view, postulating that the same cause will always lead to the same effect. Instead of trying to identify what made each "culture" unique, processualists sought to identify which mechanisms were universal for all human societies (Olsen, 1997).

The inter-relationship between human behaviour and material culture was central in processual archaeology. As opposed to culture-historical archaeologists, processual archaeologists emphasized that archaeology was a tool for reconstructing past human behaviour, not just for constructing cultural entities based on typological arrangements. By studying present day human behaviour and how it reflects in the material culture it produces, one could establish certain "rules" which could be applied for reconstructing behavioural aspects of past cultures based on the material culture they produced.

Middle range theory

Behaviour ⟵⟶ **Material culture**

However, ethno-archaeological studies showed that it was difficult, if not impossible, to identify such universal connections between behaviour and material culture. The reason is arguably that human behaviour is too complex, and is highly influenced by contextual factors. Attempting to illuminate such contextual factors led to what today is called the post-processual archaeology. A growing consensus that human behaviour was influenced by many other factors than ecological adaptation made archaeologists search for new ways of illuminating social and religious dimensions of prehistoric societies.

Thoughts ⟵⟶ Behaviour ⟵⟶ Material culture

The connection between material culture and human behaviour is very central in the current debate regarding the demise of the Neandertals. Some archaeologists argue that archaeological markers can be used in identifying the presence or absence of corresponding behavioural traits, and even the cognitive capabilities for displaying these behavioural traits (e.g. Klein 1999b). Others, inspired by Ian Hodder's "contextual" archaeology (Hodder, 1986), emphasise the importance of incorporating contextual factors, advocating that behaviour can not be directly compared across different populations and regions (e.g. McBrearty & Brooks, 2000, Henshilwood & Marean, 2003). As will be shown throughout the course of this book, one of the main sources of disagreement in the debate regarding the demise of the Neandertals is the diversified views of how the archaeological material relates to the behaviour and cognitive capabilities of those who made them (Henshilwood & Marean, 2003).

The use of negative evidence

Although numerous hypotheses regarding the nature of the Middle- to Upper Paleolithic transition exists, they can be divided into two main categories; "Discontinuists" and "Gradualists" (d'Errico & Nowell, 2000:123). Discontinuists stresses the abruptness of the transition, connecting the "revolution" (Mellars, 1994) with the migration of H. sapiens across the Eurasian plain. Central in this explanatory model is the view that Neandertals were not cognitively capable of producing the technocomplexes characterising the Upper Paleolithic. This notion is largely based on the proposed absence of advanced behavioural traits among Neandertal populations, thus it is based on negative evidence (Speth, 2004). But how appropriate is the assumption that the absence of a behavioural trait equals the absence of the ability for such behaviour? Is it not possible that not displaying a certain behavioural trait might be the result of choosing not to? Or simply not knowing how to (Speth, 2004)? Numerous factors might influence human behaviour. First, the idea that certain cognitive abilities automatically will lead to a certain type of behaviour is problematic and leans towards middle-range theory. The cause (in this case, cognitive capabilities) does not necessarily lead to the same effect (in this case, behaviour) in all contexts of the world. In fact, it would be highly unlikely. People are affected by their environment; they are affected by climate, resources, population density and ideology among other things (Henshilwood &

Marean, 2003). Second, the notion that technology, subsistence and economy related behaviour can be used as test implications for modern human cognition, implicitly suggests that all people at all times seek productive maximation, which clearly is not the case. Productive maximation is dependant upon the actual need for intensifying the exploitation of available resources among other things. As a consequence, populations living in areas with benign climatic and subsistence conditions would have a weaker incentive for new technological innovations (Foley & Lahr, 1997).

"Modern human behaviour"

Although most fields within archaeology seem to have moved away from the processual interpretation of material culture, the study of the Middle- to Upper Paleolithic transition seems still to be highly influenced by it. This is perhaps most evident in the list of behavioural traits which are believed to constitute "modern behaviour" (H. sapiens) as opposed to "archaic behaviour" (Neandertal) (Table 3.1). Postulating Neandertals as being behaviourally inferior to H. sapiens have provided a useful tool for explaining their extinction. If Neandertals were in fact unable to execute many of the behavioural traits, and by extension adaptive skills, displayed by intruding H. sapiens, their extinction would be a natural consequence of inevitably losing the putative competitive situation created by population movements and climatic fluctuations. But in later years the view of Neandertal behavioural incapability has been challenged by several authors (e.g. d'Errico, 2003, Speth, 2004).

Neandertal behavioural incapability notwithstanding, their extinction would still hinge on several other factors. Even if Neandertals were behaviourally inferior to their H. sapiens contemporaries, this would not automatically explain their extinction. Behavioural capabilities can only be considered the main factor for extinction if Neandertals and H. sapiens were in competition with one another, or if other factors (e.g. climatic fluctuations) resulted in subsistence pressure, making the putatively behaviourally "archaic" Neandertals unable to adapt. Central aspects of this ongoing discussion will be critically reviewed in proceeding chapters.

List of some of the traits used to identify "Modern Human Behaviour"	
Trait	References
Riltualized burial of the dead	Chase & Dibble, 1987, Klein, 1995, Ambrose, 1998
Personal ornamentation	Chase & Dibble, 1987, Mellars, 1989, Mithen, 1996
Non-lithic tools	Ambrose, 1998, Milo, 1998, Mellars, 1989
Blade technology	Ambrose, 1998, Foley & Lahr, 1997, Mellars 1989
Artifact standardization and diversity	Mellars, 1989, Klein, 1995
Complex hearth construction	Klein, 1995, Ambrose, 1998, Deacon, 2001
Organised use of domestic space	Klein, 1995, Ambrose, 1998, Deacon, 2001
Exploitation of marine and large mammal resources	Mellars, 1989, Milo, 1998
Seasonal mobility strategies	Klein, 1995, Milo, 1998
Use of harsh environments	Mellars, 1989, Klein, 1995, Ambrose, 1998

Table 3.1. List of traits proposed by various authors to manifest "modern" behaviour (Modified after: Henshilwood & Marean, 2003:628).

The trait list above is arguably founded on certain preconceptions:

1. All humans at all times possess a need to strive towards maximum exploitation of their ecological environment.
2. The same type of behaviour is always a result of the same cognitive capabilities and vice versa.
3. The lack of a behavioural trait directly reflects the absence of the perceived corresponding cognitive trait.

In addition, there is no consensus regarding the empirical foundation on which such a list is based. As noted by Francesco d'Errico:

> *"One can expect, for example, that a list of traits might result from a cross-cultural comparative analysis of various human societies and that the universality of a selected trait would be the criterion for its inclusion in the list. Otherwise one should accept that other researchers having a different cultural affiliation could propose features that **they** consider to define the modern experience, features which we should grant an equivalent weight"* (2003:189).

Furthermore, what is the scientific value of identifying a theoretically constructed entity called "modern human behaviour"? The scientific debate should not evolve around whether or not a certain set of behavioural traits can be characterized as "modern". It should rather concentrate on illuminating *how* people behaved, and most importantly *why* they behaved like they did. In order to do that in a satisfactory way a term like "modern human behaviour" should not be applied because the term itself pre-excludes Neandertals from processing such behavioural capabilities.

The main problem in testing such a trait list against the archaeological record is that it disregards the potentially complex nature across prehistoric societies. Human behaviour is driven by a wide range of factors, ecological adaptation being just one of them. Therefore, it is a huge paradox that researchers proclaiming to be illuminating human evolution tend to overlook the aspects which truly divide humans from other animals. If human behaviour could be studied by the same *a priory* framework as any other animal, then the field of archaeology would be superfluous.

Middle range theory

Thoughts ⟷ **Behaviour** ⟷ **Material culture**

One of the points that will be stressed in this book is that the study of Neandertals cannot be conducted merely as a biological exercise (e.g. Finlayson 2004); rather the focus should be on illuminating all aspect of Neandertal behaviour and societies.

Neandertal/H. sapiens
In order to process large amounts of information, constructing classificatory categories can be a useful tool. However, serious problems arise when such classificatory categories alternates from being a useful tool in systemising a large and often confusing empirical record to

becoming the end-goal of scientific research. Arguably, many researchers seem to find it useful to study the empirical record only to the extent of being able to fit it into a taxonomic unit. Once the artefact at hand has received an appropriate name the analysis is over. This is a practise which exhibits clear resemblance to the typological exercises of the 19th century.

"Neandertal" is a theoretical term referring to the morphologically "archaic" or "robust" hominids occupying the Eurasian plain until approximately 30 ka BP. The assumption is this particular hominid must display a certain amount of morphological "robustness" in order to qualify for the "Neandertal" title. Likewise, "H. sapiens" is the term referring to hominids displaying the same "gracile" morphological features as are present in modern human populations. However, the problem arises when this dichotomized division is applied to the empirical record. Where does "robust" end and "gracile" begin? This problem seems, in some cases, to be solved through a process of reductionism. Fossil remains are closely scrutinized and subsequently sentenced to either the "Neandertal" or "H. sapiens" condition. Although such an approach is useful in the matter of organizing the fossil remains, it represents a gross oversimplification of the factual complexity seen in morphological variations. Furthermore, several authors have suggested a close connection between biology and culture. Richard Klein argues for a mutation in the H. sapiens brain promoting modern behaviour: "Arguably, the most parsimonious explanation is the occurrence of a fortuitous, highly advantageous mutation that promoted the fully modern human brain" (Klein, 2001:9). Implicit is the suggestion that Neandertals did not experience such a mutation, thus being cognitively unable to behave "modern". The association between Neandertals and Upper Paleolithic technology is therefore explained by other parameters than technological innovativeness (e.g. Mellars, 1996, Klein, 1999a, Stringer & Gamble, 1993). When an individual is assigned to a specific hominid group, the rest of this individual's "qualities", both physically and mentally, becomes self-explanatory.

The main point to be made here is that theoretically constructed "realities" are just that; theoretically constructed. They are simplified tools constructed in order to organise large amounts of complex empirical records. The fact that archaeological material connected to Neanderthals found in for example eastern Europe, dating to 100 ka BP, would have large implications for our understanding of the Middle- to Upper Paleolithic transition in France at 40 ka BP, should tell us that our theoretical framework is grossly simplistic. Instead, seeing the empirical record as a manifestation of a mosaic interaction of contextually different hunter-gatherer groups, also affected by other parameters apart from the labels "Neanderthal" or "H. sapiens" would be more productive.

"Culture" or "Technocomplex"

Conveniently corresponding to the Neandertal/H. sapiens dichotomization, two technological entities are identified in the archaeological record; the Mousterian and the Aurignacian. Even though these terms are still very central in archaeological discussions, they were originally coined during times when archaeology was vastly different to that of today, both theoretically and methodologically, in addition to the available empirical record being vastly different. Thus, in spite of archaeology going trough major development, from the role of *fossil directeurs*, applied by Gabriel de Mortillet, to the Bordesian classificatory system (Sackett, 1981), these terms are still seen as applicable in the ever growing empirical record.

During the course of this book I will show that even though both the Aurignacian and the Mousterian are referred to as "technocomplexes" (as opposed to "cultures"), they continue to be applied, by some scholars, as if they were in fact cultures as defined by V. Gordon Childe:

> *"We find certain types of remains- pots, implements, ornaments, burial sites, house forms- constantly recurring together. Such a complex of regularly associated traits we shall term a "cultural group" or just a "culture". We assume that such a complex is the material expression of what would to-day be called a "people". Only where the complex in question is regularly and exclusively associated with skeletal remains of a specific physical type would we venture to replace "people" by the term "race"* (1929:v-vi).

As the fossil record from the earliest Upper Paleolithic is very scarce, many scholars have built their argumentation on such an association between "race" and "culture" (e.g. Mellars, 1996, Klein, 1999a, Hublin & Bailey, 2005). However, if such a direct association is not accepted, it opens for interpretations vastly different than of those of today. It is not given, *a priory*, that even thought the later occurrences of the Aurignacian was exclusively made by H. sapiens the same is true for the earliest occurrences of this technocomplex. If Neandertals were responsible for manufacturing some of the early Aurignacian sites, this would have large implications for our understanding of the late surviving Neandertals. Not only in showing that they had a much broader range of cultural and adaptive skills than previously presumed, but also in introducing the possibility of Neandertals surviving much longer than the fossil record currently indicates.

The combined results of all the theoretically biased approaches above, by and large explains the current problems seen in the debate regarding the demise of the Neandertals. As the empirical record grows bigger, both in resolution and in geographical range, is becomes more and more difficult to match it with the theoretically constructed taxonomic units. H. sapiens has frequently been found in Mousterian contexts in the Levant, and Neandertals are found in connection with blade based industries. Furthermore, the expansion of the eastern European and western Asian empirical record (discussed in chapter 6), showing that H. sapiens had little, or no role in the Middle- to Upper Paleolithic transition in these areas, implies that no simple correlation between cultural and morphological development can be established. In addition, the recent advances in radiometric dating have substantially altered the chronological framework of the fossil record. This is maybe most clearly demonstrated by the almost complete rejection of the proposed early occurrences of H. sapiens fossils in the German record (discussed in chapter 5).

Chapter 4

The environmental background during OIS 5-3 in the Eurasian areas.

Many scholars have proposed scenarios where climatic conditions contributed to the demise of Neandertals. Some of these scenarios are in direct opposition to one another, partially due to the paleoclimatic reconstructions being of low resolution (d'Errico & Sánchez Goñi, 2004). Therefore, connecting the paleoclimatic data with the archaeological- and fossil record is difficult (Mellars, 1998). The archaeological- and fossil record is also connected with dating problems (Zilhão & d'Errico, 1999, Hopkin, 2006), resulting in the demise of Neandertals being connected to both cold (Finlayson & Giles Pacheco, 2000) and warm events (Leroyer & Leroi-Gourhan, 1983). In recent years, major advancements have been made in the work of reconstructing paleoclimatic conditions (Sánchez-Goñi *et al*, 1999, 2000, 2002). The new, high-resolution reconstructions provide an improved tool for examining the role of climatic conditions on the demise of Neandertals. This chapter will provide a general presentation of the chronoclimatic framework during Oxygen Isotope Stages 5-3. The climatic framework presented in this chapter is based on three main empirical sources: 1. Oxygen isotopic ratios in deep-sea sediments. 2. Isotopic and chemical analyses of Greenland ice cores (GRIP). 3. Pollen sequences, both from pollen rich deep-sea cores and terrestrial sequences like Grande Pile Peat Bog. The numerous scenarios on climatic influence on the demise of Neandertals will be discussed in chapter 7.

100 years ago, Penck and Brückner (1909) suggested a Pleistocene chronology divided into four glacial periods, Günz, Mindel, Riss and Würm. Today, this scenario has been replaced by a far more complicated pattern of warm and cold periods. Some of these periods lasted for a long time and had a major impact on contemporary faunal and floral conditions, while other periods were short and had a smaller impact on terrestrial conditions. The long lasting warm and cold periods are called interglacials and glacials respectively, while shorter warm and cold periods are referred to as interstadials and stadials respectively. Geneviève Woillard characterizes the difference between interstadials and interglacials as follows:

"An interglacial (...) represents an important warming characterized by a vegetational evolution which presents a logical succession from an ecological point of view. This

succession of vegetation landscapes, from very cold types to the climax forest, followed by the return of cold forests (...), is found during each interglacial with variations of only minor importance (...) An interstadial (...) represents a shorter and less-marked warming which has not allowed thermophilous species to immigrate again from their refuge in successive well-ordered waves" (Woillard, 1978:15).

The exact definition of "stadials" and "interstadials" is however controversial. While some researchers use the definition applied by Woillard, others apply a relative definition of these terms, indicating climatic amelioration or deterioration relative to preceding periods. Such a relative definition however, would result in some "interstadial" conditions being similar to "stadial" conditions of other time periods (Behre, 1989). Archaeologically, the most important factors to be considered are the climatic impact on the contemporary humans. The climatic oscillations in themselves would therefore arguably be of major importance because it involves the need for a shift in adaptation. Therefore, the relative definition of these terms will be applied in this book.

Oxygen Isotope Stages

The sediments of the ocean floor contain a large amount of skeletal remains of microscopic animals called "foraminifera". When these animals were alive they lived at the ocean surface and accumulated two isotopes of oxygen, ^{18}O and ^{16}O. Because ^{16}O is lighter than ^{18}O, the water locked up on land in ice caps during cold periods will contain larger amounts of ^{16}O relative to the water left in the ocean (Stringer & Gamble, 1993). This will affect the oxygen isotope ratio taken up by foraminifera while still alive. By using a mass spectrometer to examine the $^{18}O/^{16}O$ ratio in each foraminifera specimen from deep-sea sediments, Cesare Emiliani pioneered the possibilities for reconstructing past climatic sequences (Emiliani, 1955). Emiliani connected the varying oxygen isotope ratios to ocean temperature variations, and his examinations revealed a repeated pattern of interglacial and glacial climates. Based on these results Emiliani identified 14 separate isotopic stages, interglacial stages represented by odd numbers and glacial stages represented by even numbers. Later absolute dating of deep-sea cores, like V28-238, has show that Emiliani's original stages were remarkably precise, with the exception of stage 14 which were shown to be ca 200,000 years older than his estimate (Stringer & Gamble, 1993).

Later methodological and theoretical advances led Nicholas Shackleton among others further refined the procedures of examining oxygen isotopic ratios in foraminifera. Perhaps the most important discovery by Shackleton was that these ratios were, contrary to Emiliani's view, not predominantly affected by sea-water temperature directly, but by the total volume of the ocean water relative to the water locked up on land in the form of ice caps (Shackleton, 1987, Shackleton & Opdyke, 1973). This discovery arguably made the oxygen isotope ratios more closely connected to climatic variations, because they not only reflected conditions in the ocean itself but were also influenced by terrestrial factors like the size of ice caps and sea level (Shackleton, 1967).

The late Pleistocene climatic sequence has been far better researched than preceding periods. The examination of hundreds of different deep-sea cores and many detailed pollen sequences has revealed a pattern of relatively rapid climatic oscillations between warm and cold phases (d'Errico & Sánchez Goñi, 2003). The last glacial cycle does not only constitute one interglacial and one glacial period, higher resolution research has revealed a much more complicated scenario. The saw-toothed curve published by Dansgaard, *et al.* (1993) indicates a climatic cycle (last interglacial and glacial) which by no means was characterized by a linear development from mild benign climates during the "Eemian" period to cold and harsh climates during the last glacial maximum. This period was characterized by short climatic episodes lasting from 500-2000 years, and the shift between some of them might not have taken longer than about 100 years (Johnsen *et al*, 1992). These rapid oscillations would arguably have a major impact on the contemporary human habitants, because the abrupt nature of the oscillations would not allow a time-demanding adaptive adjustment.

The last interglacial

There is a general agreement that the last interglacial (Eemian) is restricted to oxygen isotope stage (OIS) 5e, ca. 126,000 to 118,000 BP (Mellars, 1996, Dansgaard et al, 1993). One of the most characteristic features of the last interglacial is the abrupt nature of its appearance. The immediately preceding period, OIS- 6, was an extremely cold period, probably almost as cold as during the last glacial maximum at 18,000 BP. The OIS-5e commenced with temperatures rising at least 10-15°C within a time period of ca 5000 years (Martinson et al, 1987). Ecological reconstructions based on detailed pollen records indicate a sequence which was initiated by the growth of cold adapted tree species like birch and pine. After this initial stage there was a succession of deciduous species that required warm conditions, with a subsequent reversion to coniferous species at the later stages of this period (Zagwijn, 1990). When compared to present day, the last interglacial was a world dominated by megafauna. Subtropical conditions as far north as the British Isles supported species like hippopotami, straight-tusked elephants and narrow-nosed rhinoceroses (Stringer & Gamble, 1993).

Early glacial period

The early glacial period constitutes OIS 5d, 5c, 5b and 5a, from ca 118,000 to 75,000 BP. This period is characterized by a complex pattern of climatic oscillations. OIS-5d and OIS-5b, called "Melisey I" and "Melisey II" respectively were cold periods (Shackleton, 1977). During these periods the polar front extended southwards to the latitude of approximately 52 $^{\circ}$N, which correlates roughly to the latitude of southern England (Mellars, 1996). From the pollen sequence at Grande Pile, Geneviève Woillard found that the vegetation in OIS-5d and OIS-5b was dominated by steppic plants like Artemisia, Chenopodiaceae, Thalicritum and Compositae (Woillard, 1978). There is also evidence that hardier tree species like birch, pine and willow survived in patches in some areas, predominantly towards the south and east corners of the continent (Zagwijn, 1990). This suggests that the climate during Melisey I and II never became as severe as it was during the later fully glacial periods of oxygen isotope stages 4 and 2 (Mellars, 1996).

Perhaps the most striking feature of the OIS-5 is the relative warmth of the OIS-5c and OIS-5a interstadials, called St. Germain I and II, respectively. The oxygen isotope ratios indicate that the ice mass volume was reduced to approximately half the size of the 5d and 5b periods (Shackleton, 1987). Consequently the polar front retreated to a latitude of about 60 $^{\circ}$N. The vegetational sequence at Grande Pile shows a similar pattern as the Eemian interglacial, characterized by an initial stage of subarctic tundra landscapes, followed by a succession of deciduous forests requiring warm conditions (Woillard, 1978). However, as indicated by Karl Ernst Behre (1989) the biostratigraphy of Europe in this period is geographically highly differentiated.

Oxygen isotope stage 4

The middle glacial period was initiated by the onset of OIS 4, dated to ca. 75,000-60,000 BP (Martinson *et al*, 1987). OIS-4 is characterized by a far more rigorous climate than the immediately preceding OIS-5a. The oxygen isotope ratios reveal a major expansion of the polar front, probably to 45 $^{\circ}$N, almost, as far south as during the last glacial maximum at

18,000 BP (Mellars, 1996). This rapid decline in temperature led to a reversal of the forest vegetation and the successive spread of steppe/tundra vegetation (Behre, 1989). Correspondingly, the Neandertal (Mousterian) site distribution during this period is confined south of the 45 °N latitude, with only 12 sites recovered dating to this period (van Andel *et al*, 2003).

Oxygen isotope stage 3

OIS-3 is dated from ca. 60,000 to 25,000 BP (Mellars, 1996), thus covering the entire period from when anatomically modern humans first appeared in Europe until the last Neandertals disappeared from the archaeological record. Several hypotheses regarding the climatic and ecological influence on the demise of the Neandertals have been suggested (e.g. Leroyer & Leroi-Gourhan, 1983, Mellars, 1998, Finlayson, 2004, Gamble, 2004). As indicated by SPECMAP, OIS-3 was a predominantly mild phase between OIS-4 and OIS-2 (Imbrie *et al*, 1984). As mentioned earlier in this chapter, the SPECMAP time-scale is based on ^{18}O and ^{16}O ratios in ocean waters, indicating the total mass of water bound on land in form of ice, relative to the ocean volume (Davies, *et al*, 2000). The process of accumulating ice sheets is relatively slow, making the SPECMAP a low-resolution sequence. However, high resolution ice core studies from Summit, central Greenland, the so-called "GRIP" and GISP2 projects (Bond *et al*, 1993, Dansgaard *et al*, 1993, Grootes *et al*, 1993, Johnsen *et al*, 1992 and GRIP Members, 1993), has shown that OIS-3 is a period which is characterized by a high frequency of climatic oscillations called Dansgaard-Oeschger stadials and interstadials (Dansgaard, *et al*, 1993). The Dansgaard-Oeschger interstadials average temperatures were a mere 2°C below local mean temperatures in the Holocene. Dansgaard-Oeschger stadials had temperatures close to those of the last glacial maximum (Barron & Pollard, 2002). The interstadials lasted some millennia, but the stadials lasted for a few centuries, and the transition between warm and cold events could take as little as a few decades (van Andel, 2002).

Heinrich events

Hartmut Heinrich (1988) discovered sediments in the eastern part of the northern Atlantic containing unusually high ratios of ice-rafted lithic fragments relative to foraminifera shells. These layers appeared with intervals of roughly 10,000 years (Broecker *et al*, 1992). The Heinrich layers have been interpreted as indicating short periods of intense iceberg discharge from the region around the Hudson Strait (Hemming, 2004). Reaching warm waters in the northeast Atlantic resulted in the ice melting and releasing ice-rafted detritus (Cayre *et al*,

1999), in addition to 100-400 km^3 of water, reducing the salinity of the surface waters in the North Atlantic. Such a reduced salinity would effect the movements of ocean currents, creating so-called "Bond cycles" (Bond *et al*, 1993). Such cycles would furthermore result in rapid cooling events represented by Dansgaard-Oeschger stadials (Hemming, 2004). Six so-called Heinrich Events (HE) (Broecker *et al*, 1992) have been identified within the last 70 000 years. However, the exact effect of the Heinrich events on terrestrial conditions is still poorly known (Sánchez Goñi *et al*, 2000). The largest event is HE 4 dated to 38 ka BP based on correlation to the GISP2 record (Meese *et al*, 1997), and is of special interest here because it might have had large implications for Neandertal and H. sapiens subsistence during the Middle- to Upper Paleolithic transition. As noted by d'Errico and Sánchez-Goñi (2003), nowhere in Europe are Mousterian sites AMS dated within the H4 event. The same is the case for the Aurignacian sites in southern Iberia, indicating that this area was scarcely inhabited during the H4 event. This population pattern might be due to changes in the subsistence during H4. During the cold phases of OIS 3, large Mammals were sustained by the grasslands of Northern Iberia, while the desert-steppe environments forming in southern Iberia were unable to feed large Mammals, resulting in low biomass is these areas (d'Errico & Sánchez-Goñi, 2003).

Most of the climatic oscillations in OIS-3 were too brief to show up in most of the climatic records like the deep-sea core oxygen isotope sequences and most of the terrestrial pollen sequences. This might be due to the oscillations not having a strong enough impact on the environment to show up in these sequences. But it might also be due to these sequences not being of high enough resolution to detect brief oscillations of the environment. The Oerel, Glinde, Hengelo and Denekamp interstadials are relatively long lasting warming events, approximately 2,000-4,000 years (Mellars, 1996), long enough to be detected in arboreal pollen excursions like Grande Pile (Behre, 1989, Woillard, 1978), and are recorded both in Northern and Southern Europe (Davies *et al*, 2000). The Hengelo interstadial (Fig. 4.2) is of special interest because it broadly dates to the same time-period as the Middle- to Upper Paleolithic transition, 40-37 ka BP (d'Errico & Sánchez Goñi, 2003). However, correlating climatic evidence with the archaeological record has proven difficult as a result of low geographical and chronological resolution, both in the climatic- and archaeological record (Davies *et al.* 2000).

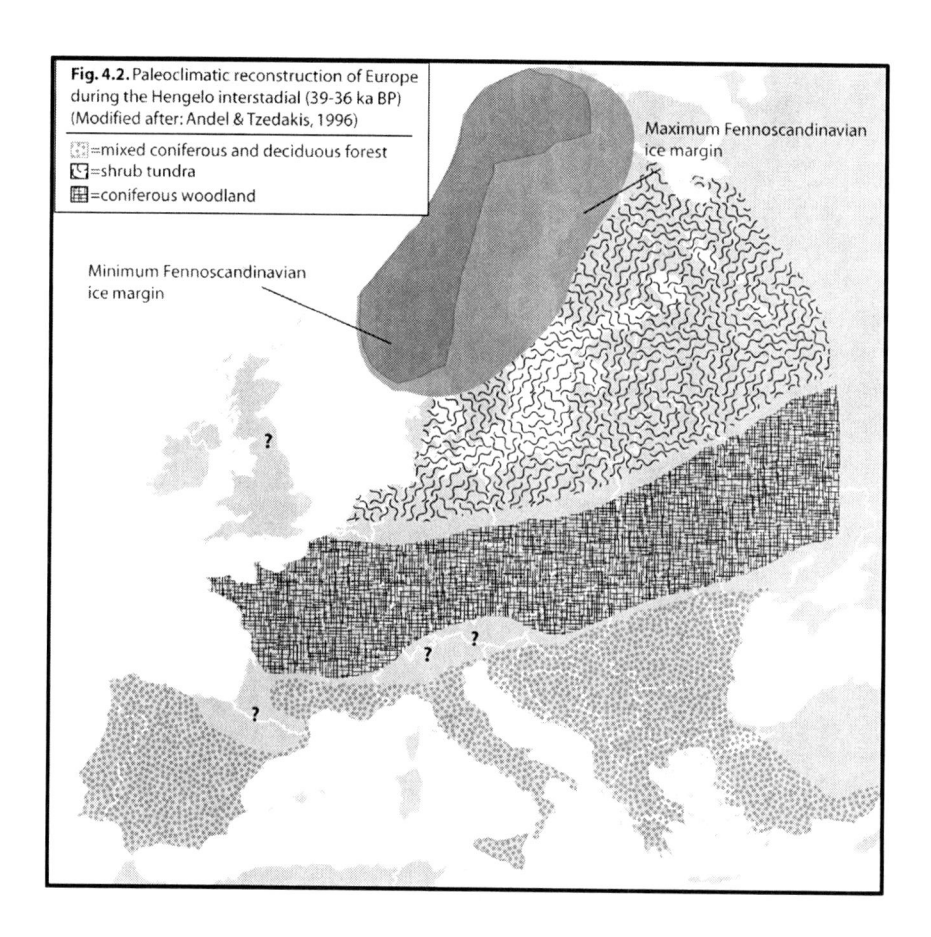

Fig. 4.2. Paleoclimatic reconstruction of Europe during the Hengelo interstadial (39-36 ka BP) (Modified after: Andel & Tzedakis, 1996)

= mixed coniferous and deciduous forest
= shrub tundra
= coniferous woodland

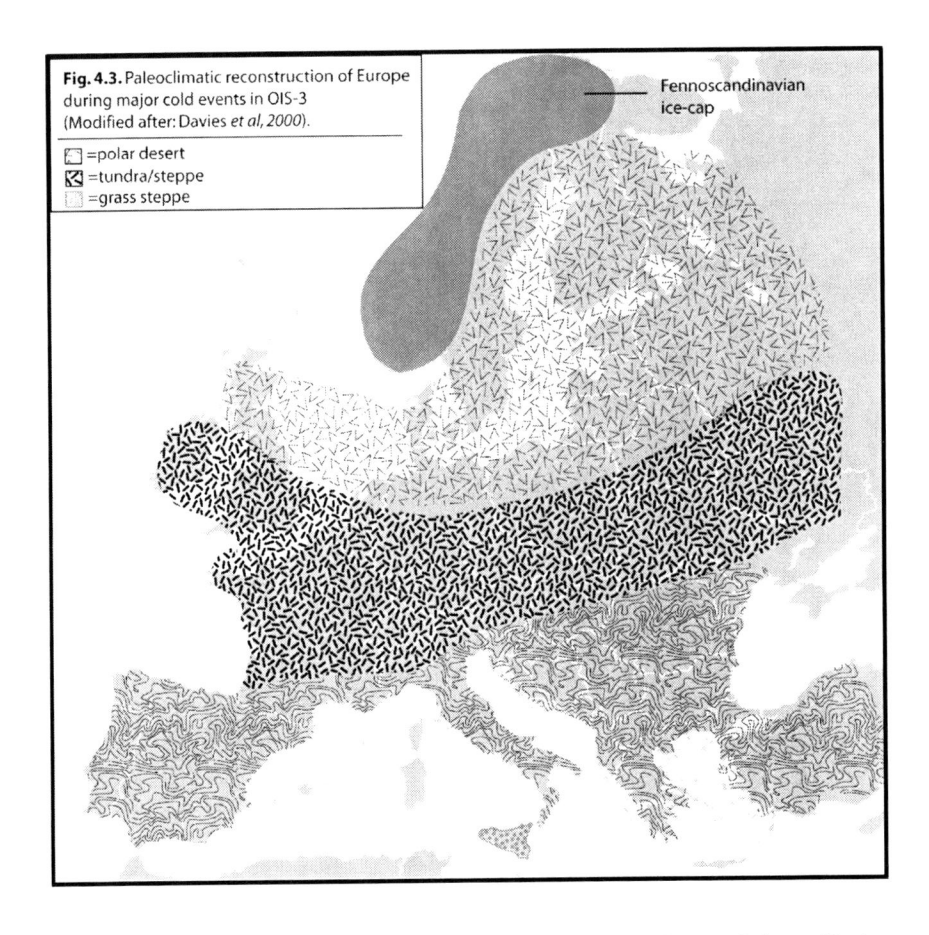

Fig. 4.3. Paleoclimatic reconstruction of Europe during major cold events in OIS-3 (Modified after: Davies *et al*, 2000).

- = polar desert
- = tundra/steppe
- = grass steppe

Fennoscandinavian ice-cap

Archaeologically, climatic conditions are only of interest to the degree of them effecting ecological conditions, and thereby human occupation and behaviour. The Grande Pile and Les Echets pollen sequences from Eastern France are two of the best available sequences for illuminating the vegetation, and by extension faunal development during OIS-3. These pollen sequences show that the Hengelo interstadial represents a climatic amelioration leading to shrub tundra development (Behre, 1989). The Hengelo interstadial was thus a non-forest interstadial unlike preceding interstadials like OIS-5c and OIS-5a. This indicates that even though OIS-3 was characterized by a milder climate relative to OIS-4, this stage was never comparable with the benign conditions of preceding interstadials characterized by full coniferous forests (Behre & van der Plicht, 1992, Gómez-Orellana *et al*, 2007).

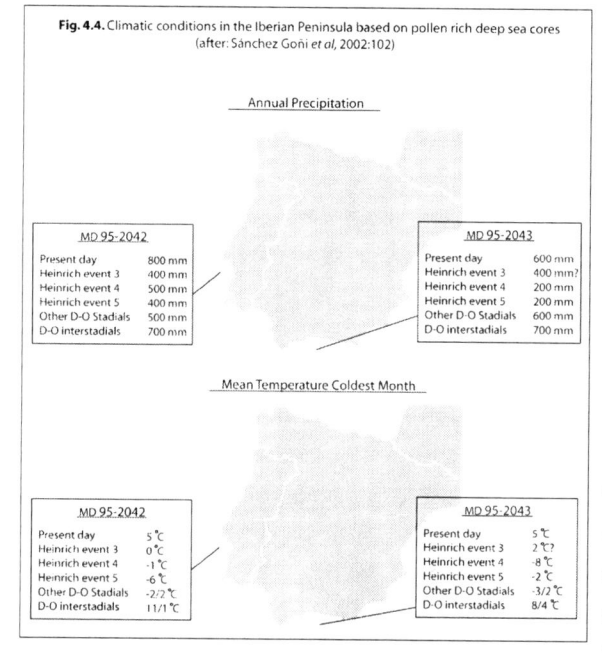

Fig. 4.4. Climatic conditions in the Iberian Peninsula based on pollen rich deep sea cores (after: Sánchez Goñi et al, 2002:102)

Annual Precipitation

MD 95-2042	
Present day	800 mm
Heinrich event 3	400 mm
Heinrich event 4	500 mm
Heinrich event 5	400 mm
Other D-O Stadials	500 mm
D-O interstadials	700 mm

MD 95-2043	
Present day	600 mm
Heinrich event 3	400 mm?
Heinrich event 4	200 mm
Heinrich event 5	200 mm
Other D-O Stadials	600 mm
D-O interstadials	700 mm

Mean Temperature Coldest Month

MD 95-2042	
Present day	5 °C
Heinrich event 3	0 °C
Heinrich event 4	-1 °C
Heinrich event 5	-6 °C
Other D-O Stadials	-2/2 °C
D-O interstadials	11/1 °C

MD 95-2043	
Present day	5 °C
Heinrich event 3	2 °C?
Heinrich event 4	-8 °C
Heinrich event 5	-2 °C
Other D-O Stadials	-3/2 °C
D-O interstadials	8/4 °C

Pollen rich marine cores

As a result of the current uncertainties of radiometric dating methods within this time period, it is very difficult to establish a firm correlation between the climatic proxy data recorded in the deep-sea oxygen isotope sequences, Greenland ice-cores and terrestrial pollen sequences. This problem might be solved by analysing pollen sequences from deep-sea cores. Two pollen rich marine cores have been obtained from the coast of the Iberian Peninsula, MD95-2042 located near the south-western margin of the Peninsula (Sánchez Goñi *et al*, 2000), and MD95-2043 in the Alborean Sea (Sánchez Goñi *et al*, 2002).

These cores indicate close correlations between the Dansgaard-Oeschger oscillations recorded in the Greenland ice core and the vegetational development in the Iberian Peninsula (Sánchez Goñi *et al*, 1999). A three-phase pattern of each Heinrich event in land and ocean environments can be seen in these high resolution sequences. The first and last phase of Heinrich Event 4 was characterized by mild and humid climate in south-western Europe, while the middle part represented a cold and dry climate (Sánchez Goñi *et al*, 2000). The two pollen rich deep-sea cores also revealed a different environmental impact of the Heinrich Events than that during the other Dansgaard-Oeschger stadials. While a similar pattern of precipitation and temperature drops is evident for the entire Iberian Peninsula for most of the Dansgaard-Oeschger stadials, the Heinrich Events show a diversified impact for the Atlantic and Mediterranean sides. While the Heinrich Events are related to a strong influence of the Scandinavian Mobile Polar High (MPH), the other Dansgaard-Oeschger stadials may have been influenced by the Atlantic MPH (Sánchez Goñi *et al*, 2002). The cores show that while the Atlantic MPH mostly would influence the terrestrial environments of the Atlantic margin of the Iberian Peninsula, the Scandinavian MPH would have a similar impact on the entire Peninsula. As a result, the conditions during Heinrich Events would be far more diversified in the two areas of the Peninsula than during other stadials. During Heinrich Event 4, this would result in an annual precipitation 300 mm higher in the western margin than in the Mediterranean areas and 200 mm during Heinrich Event 5 (Fig. 4.3). The relative conditions during Heinrich Event 5 would therefore be in accordance to the present day precipitation gradient in these areas (Sánchez Goñi et al, 2002).

The high resolution pattern of terrestrial response to climatic oscillation is in direct opposition to the hypothesis of a relatively stable environment in the Mediterranean areas during OIS-3 (d'Errico & Sánchez Goñi, 2003, van Andel et al, 2003). However, as noted by Carrión (2004) two marine pollen records are not enough to discard the studies of pollen assemblages from both lakes, peatbogs and cave sediments which shows a much more stationary character of the Mediterranean region. Notwithstanding, the pollen rich sequences obtained from deep-sea cores represent a unique possibility for establishing direct high resolution marine-terrestrial correlations. Obtaining palynological data from anthropological sites is associated with serious sources of error (Bryant & Hall, 1993). Being able to create a correlation between marine and terrestrial environmental data, without the wide-spread reliance on palynological data from archaeological sites, would therefore be preferable. In addition to more reliable correlations, these cores may provide a higher resolution, both in time and space, of the paleoenvironmental framework. Such a high resolution is crucial in any attempt to connect this information to the archaeological and anthropological data within a chronological framework.

Vegetational development in the Iberian Peninsula during OIS-3
Environmental conditions in the Iberian Peninsula during OIS-3 are of special interest when examining the demise of the Neandertal because they survived in these areas much longer than in the rest of Europe (Zilhão, 2000). The pollen sequences of both pollen rich deep-sea cores identify 19-20 climatic phases corresponding to the Dansgaard-Oeschger stadials and interstadials (Sánchez Goñi et al, 2002). During cold/dry phases the vegetation developed towards desert-steppe vegetation, although small pockets of trees would survive in mid- and low altitudes. During mild/wet periods there were a succession of deciduous woodland with Mediterranean trees and shrubs (d'Errico & Sánchez Goñi, 2003). As mentioned above, the

Heinrich Events would have a larger impact on the Mediterranean side of the Peninsula than would other Dansgaard-Oeschger stadials. Therefore, during Heinrich Events the desert-steppe vegetation would reach a larger distribution area than it would during regular Dansgaard-Oeschger stadials.

Neandertal occupation patterns in Eurasia during OIS-3

The initial stages of OIS-3 (59-44 ka BP), was characterised by a long warming with occasional interrupting cold events (Barron *et al*, 2003). As opposed to OIS-4, which was characterised by relatively few sites, confined south of 45 °N latitude, the initial stages of OIS-3 was characterised by a marked increase of recovered sites as well as an expansion northwards to approximately 50 °N latitude (van Andel *et al*, 2003). After 43 ka BP, as the climate started to deteriorate, Neandertals once again retreated southwards, although the number of sites recovered is similar to that of the earlier stages of OIS-3 (van Andel, 2003). At 40 ka BP, four absence zones appear in England, Eastern Europe, northern Italy and north-western Spain (Bocquet-Appel & Demars, 2000). The occupation pattern from 37 ka BP onwards show a clear pattern of reduction in the total number of Mousterian sites in addition to a continued retreat into southern refugia, corresponding with the gradually deteriorating climate towards the Last Glacial Maximum (van Andel *et al*, 2003). At approximately 30 ka BP, there are only two relatively small areas with Neandertal occupations visible in the empirical record; southern France (north of the Alps) and the south-western areas of the Iberian Peninsula (Bocquet-Appel & Demars, 2000).

Chapter 5

Interbreeding, continuity or total replacement?

Neandertals no longer exist as a morphological type. While some argue that these morphological features simply disappeared due to evolution towards morphological modernity, others claim that they disappeared as a result of being replaced by intruding H. sapiens from the African continent. Within both these explanation models, different degrees of admixture between the two contemporary, but morphologically different hominid groups have been advocated. Although the study of recent human evolution is often dichotomized into two camps, there is in fact a wide range of explanatory models, each advocating their own interpretation of the empirical record (Fig. 5.1). This chapter will review the currently dominating theories regarding the nature of the disappearance of morphologically archaic Neandertals, with emphasis on the fossil record.

The Recent African Origins (RAO) Model
Although most researchers agree on the spread of *Homo erectus* from Africa across the old world during the Lower- or early Middle Pleistocene (the so-called "Out of Africa 1"), the current debate is concentrated on whether or not a similar scenario took place in association with the appearance of H. sapiens. Proponents of the RAO model, argue that all present day humans have a common place of origin within the African continent (e.g. Stringer, 2002a, Mellars, 2006b,). Modern-looking morphological features evolved exclusively in Africa between 150,000 and 100,000 years ago, subsequently spreading out of the African continent, replacing all "archaic" populations across the Old World. Central in this model is the view of Neandertals becoming extinct with little or no contribution to the prevailing gene pool (Stringer, 1989, Vandermeersch, 1989, Mellars, 1996, Klein 1999a, 2003). Neandertals and H. sapiens are by advocates of the RAO models seen as different biological species, thus unable to interbreed significantly (Stringer & Andrews, 1988).

In the early 1960's, Louis Leakey argued, strictly based on morphological features, that hominids living in Africa during the Lower- or early Middle Pleistocene were more likely to be the ancestors to modern humans than their *Homo erectus* contemporaries from the Far East (Leakey, 1963). Based on cladistic methodology, several other studies supported Leakey's

As seen above, most explanatory models, advocate some degree of interbreeding between Neandertals and H. sapiens. Even the strongest proponents of the RAO hypothesis do not rule out the possibility for individual cases of interbreeding, although insignificant in the evolutionary development (Stringer, 2002b). However, the general scarcity of fossil remains from the crucial period of contact between Neandertals and H. sapiens has hitherto prohibited satisfactory empirical evidence, either confirming or refuting hybridisation as a widespread practise.

The ≈4-year-old child fossil found at Abrigo do Lagar Velho in Portugal is one of the few putative hybrid remains discovered. This hominid fossil was recovered in a burial context, with ochre stained sediments and a pierced *Littorina obtusata* shell, showing close resemblance to Gravettian burials across Europe (Duarte *et al*, 1999). AMS dating of charcoal directly associated with the burial yielded a result of ca. 24.5 ka BP. Detailed examinations of the fossil remains, revealed morphological traits associated with both Neandertal and H. sapiens variations, and Duarte *et al.* (1999) classified the 4-year-old as a possible hybrid between Neandertals and H. sapiens. The strongest points of objection in regards to this conclusion are that of chronology, the fragmentary nature of the cranium (Tattersall & Schwartz, 1999), and the premature age of the specimen (Stringer, 2002b). The time gap between the proposed hybrid at Lagar Velho and the time at which the Neandertals were thought to have disappeared is several thousand years. However, the newly dated Mousterian tools at Gorham's Cave (~28 ka BP) (Finlayson *et al.* 2006), Gibraltar, strengthen the possibility of a relatively long Neandertal and H. sapiens period of contact in southern Iberia. If the youngest dates from Finlayson *et al.* (~24 ka BP) were to be accepted, this would further compliment the conclusion of the Lagar Velho being a hybrid. The youngest dates from Gorham's Cave should however be treated with caution because they are associated with stratigraphic inconsistencies (Delson & Harvati, 2006). The actual phylogenetic history of the Lagar Velho child is still a controversial issue (Balter, 2001). Although a lot of progress has been made on the examination of this specimen and its cultural context (Trinkhaus & Zilhão, 2002), there are still many problems that needs to be solved before the Lagar Velho fossil can provide compelling evidence regarding Neandertal/H. sapiens admixture.

DNA analysis

Any trace of Neandertal mitochondrial DNA (mtDNA) is absent, or at least currently undetectable from the present day human gene pool (Cann *et al*, 1987, Stoneking & Cann, 1989, Vigilant *et al*, 1991, Serre *et al*, 2004). Comparative studies of modern human and Neandertal DNA suggest a long period of separate development between Neandertals and H. sapiens, somewhere between 300,000 and 750,000 years (Krings *et al*, 1997, Beerli & Edwards, 2002, Pääbo *et al*, 2004, Green *et al*, 2006). However, the absence of Neandertal genetic traces in extant populations has also been argued to be the result of genetic drift (Zilhão, 2006a). This issue has recently been addressed by studies of aDNA from H. sapiens fossil samples dating broadly from the same time period as the last Neandertals (Serre *et al*, 2004). Due to a general lack of available fossil remains of H. sapiens from this time period combined with significant methodological problems, such studies operate with a high degree of uncertainties. Nonetheless, the currently available empirical record suggests that Neandertals did not contribute to the present day gene pool. Why Neandertal DNA did not prevail up to the extant gene pool however, may be due to numerous factors, not interbreeding with H. sapiens being just one of them.

The question of hybridisation resulting in viable offspring hinges on whether or not Neandertals should be considered a distinctive species or a H. sapiens subspecies. Studies of pairwise sequence differences between Neandertal and modern human DNA show that there are considerable differences between them. Neandertals have three times as many differences relative to modern humans than living day populations have between themselves (Krings *et al*, 1999). Furthermore, the Neandertal mtDNA sequences are closer related to one another, than to modern human mtDNA (Green *et al*, 2006). However, as noted by Relethford (2001) the relatively large differences between Neandertals and H. sapiens does not surpass the differences seen between 2 out of 3 chimpanzee subspecies. Furthermore, the Neandertal samples used in the analysis spanned tens of thousands of years, thus potentially displaying larger variation than it would from a single point in time (Relethford, 2001).

Although there is a general consensus that the ancestry of all present day humans can be traced back to African populations prior to the "Out of Africa 2" event, there is a lively debate regarding the potential Neandertal contribution to the present day human gene pool during the Middle- to Upper Paleolithic transition (Zilhão, 2006a, Relethford, 2001). Which degree of admixing could potentially have taken place without Neandertal mtDNA traces being present view (Stringer *et al.* 1984, Bräuer, 1984). Advances in genetic analysis also provided increased evidence for all modern day population having a common ancestor in Africa (Cann *et al.* 1987). As it became evident that Neandertal mtDNA is not detectable within the extant genetic lineages, proponents of the RAO model argued that this supported the view of a migrating population replacing the Neandertals, without significant contribution to the contemporary H. sapiens gene pool. An important aspect of the RAO model is the view of the morphological gap between Neandertals and H. sapiens being too big to be bridged by *in situ* evolution during the short time period between the last Neandertals and the early H. sapiens, in addition to late Neandertal fossils not displaying directional change towards anatomical modernity (Stringer, 1992b). The RAO model argues for the fossil record displaying an abruptness between the Middle- and Upper Paleolithic only explainable through population migration and replacement.

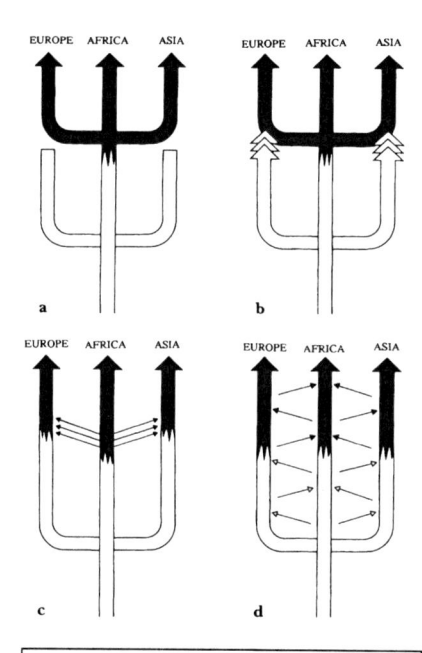

Fig. 5.1. Comparison between the main four competing models regarding the demise of the Neandertals. (a) Recent African Origin; (b) Hybridization and Replacement; (c) Assimilation; (d) Multiregional Evolution (Aiello, 1993).

The Hybridization and Replacement Model
As with the RAO model, proponents of the Hybridization and Replacement model, advocate a scenario where H. sapiens migrated out of Africa. But contrary to the RAO, this model promotes higher degree of hybridization between local Neandertals and migrating H. sapiens, subsequently resulting in the extinction of the Neandertals (e.g. Bräuer, 1984). This model deviates from the Assimilation model in that although it recognises some degree of hybridisation, the most important factor for the origin of anatomically modern Europeans is the migrating African population (Bräuer, 1989).

Multiregional evolution
Multiregionalists reject the view of a single place of origin for all modern day humans. Instead, they emphasise the importance of regional evolution resulting from adaptation to local conditions. The Eurasian record is thus

interpreted as showing an *in situ* development from Neandertal- to modern morphology. Central to this theory is the emphasis on intra-specific variation in Neandertal morphology, indicating the development towards anatomical modernity. Implicit in the Multiregional model is the assumption that variations observed in present day populations originated from regional development within *Homo erectus* due to different adaptive environments. The fact that the proposed regional development of *Homo erectus* did not result in multiple present day human races, is explained by inter-population gene flow. Multiregionalists also divide a species geographical range into two zones; "The polytypic center" and "The monomorphic periphery" (Wolpoff *et al*, 1984:452). Due to populations being larger (and thereby genetically more sustainable) in the polytypic centre (the area where the species originally evolved), than in the periphery of the species geographical range, populations close to the geographical centre will display more morphological variation than the peripheral populations (Templeton, 1982).

The Assimilation Model

The Assimilation model was first proposed by Smith *et al.* (1989). Although this model also accepts an African origin for modern humans, it emphasises the importance of gene flow, hybridizations and other factors resulting in directional morphological change. Implicit in this model is the view that population migration did not play a crucial role in the appearance of H. sapiens, at least not in all regions of the world (Smith *et al*, 2005). Advocates of the Assimilation model do not accept that Neandertals can unequivocally be described as a separate hominid species, thus applying the terms "archaic" and "modern" H. sapiens, instead of "H. sapiens" and "H. neanderthalensis" (Smith *et al*, 1989).

The fossil evidence

The application of thermoluminescence (TL) and electron spin resonance (ESR) dating from the end of the 1980's onwards, as well as improvement in the Potassium-Argon dating method during the 1970's (Curtis, 1975), has produced overwhelming evidence of H. sapiens morphology being present in Africa approximately 100,000 years before detectable in Europe (White *et al*, 2003, Fleagle *et al*, 2003). In the Levant, H. sapiens seems to be present some 60,000 years earlier than in Europe (Grün & Stringer, 1991, Valladas *et al*, 1988). Although this has been cited as compelling evidence against multiregional evolution, it does not exclude the possibility for the same evolutionary processes, apparently taking place in Africa approximately 160 ka BP, to have happened in Europe some 100,000 years later. Some differences between the African and Eurasian record can however not be ignored. As opposed to the Eurasian record, the African record does not display a chronological overlap between anatomically archaic and modern populations. A situation with potential direct contact between anatomically archaic and modern populations seems to be strictly confined to the Eurasian record, a central point when elaborating the suitability of using the Eurasian record as the empirical basis in establishing a global-scale evolutionary hypothesis (Henshilwood & Marean, 2003, d'Errico, 2003).

Assessing the question of *in situ* evolution or population replacement based on the fossil record, hinges on the determination of whether morphological "anomalies" represent pathological, evolutionary or intra-specific variation, or actual hybridization. Although generally, Neandertal and H. sapiens morphological features are distinctly different, there are exceptions, both with regard to Neandertal fossils displaying modern features, and H. sapiens displaying archaic features. One of the first to apply a detailed research on the range of Neandertal morphology was Aleš Hrdlička, who interpreted the empirical record as illuminating changes in Neandertal morphology through time, and towards them becoming modern-looking:

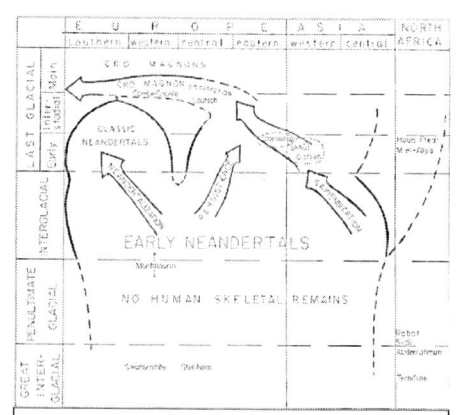

Fig. 5.2. Howell's illustration of the division between two different Neandertal types, and the admixture between Neandertals and H. sapiens in the Levant. (1957:432).

"*The Neanderthal form is a necessary stage of man's evolution; it is not uniform in type either as to the skull or skeleton; it shows plain indications of progressive differentiation towards modern man; and is met with in a more or less dilute but still recognizable form in later humanity, even down to the present day*" (Hrdlička, 1926:151).

Later proponents of *in situ* evolution tend to stress the lack of a uniform type of Neandertal morphology. Perhaps most famous is Clark Howells visualisation of the divergence between "classic" Neandertals of south-western Europe and Neandertals displaying more gracile features in other areas of

43

Eurasia (Fig. 5.2). C. Loring Brace also stressed the difficulties in defining Neandertal morphology:

> "*In fact, in the two instances where remains of 10 or more individuals have been found-Krapina and Mount Carmel-the range of variation is embarrassingly great for the proponents of the "uniform type" picture.*" (1962:730).

The late Neandertals from Vindija Cave in Croatia have long been central in this discussion. Intermediate morphology, like reduction in the anterior tooth size, nasal narrowing and more anterior position of the mental foramen has been proposed (Wolpoff *et al*, 1981). Relative to the morphology of the earlier remains from Krapina; the Vindija remains show a development towards anatomical modernity. The same conclusion is reached when browridge development is compared between the early Mousterian (Krapina), late Mousterian (Vindija) and early Upper Paleolithic (Velika Pećina) remains; showing a pattern of reduction in browridge size (Frayer *et al*, 1993). However, the analysis undertaken by Frayer *et al.* was subsequently criticised for being biased, based on different age and/or sex compositions between the samples (Ahern *et al*, 2002). Furthermore, the Velika Pećina remains are no longer pertinent in this discussion due to recent redating placing it at approximately 5 ka BP (Smith *et al*, 1999).

The late Neandertal fossil from Saint-Césaire also displays certain morphological features consistent with *in situ* evolution. As noted by Wolpoff and Frayer (1992), the Saint-Césaire Neandertal anterior tooth size is in closer resemblance to early H. sapiens, than early H. sapiens and late Upper Paleolithic specimens. Chris Stringer on the other hand, emphasise other morphological features, such as midfacial projection, leading him to conclude that "Saint-Césaire deviates in the direction away from early modern European values" (1992b:201). The diametrically opposing conclusions drawn from the same fossil evidence at Saint-Césaire, clearly demonstrates the difficulty of creating an unequivocal Neandertal morphological definition, and the resulting difficulties in establishing a chronological framework of Neandertal morphological development. Establishing a secure chronological development based purely on fossil remains would require an enormous amount of available data. Therefore, DNA analysis of both extant and ancient genetic material has proved a useful tool in supplementing the information available from fossil remains, and will be discussed later in this chapter.

among extant humans? Several assessments have been made in this regard. Serre *et al.* (2004) suggested a maximum of 25% admixing without Neandertal mtDNA being visible in present day populations. However, as noted by Serre *et al.* (2004) and others (Cooper *et al*, 2004, Zilhão, 2006a), such estimations are dependent on a number of assumptions. One factor which would substantially affect this estimation is the time at which the proposed admixing took place. A large deviation between the five H. sapiens lineages examined by Serre *et al.* (2004) at approximately 25 ka BP and the admixing event would significantly enlarge the potential percentage of Neandertal contribution. The fossil evidence ascribed by Serre *et al.* (2004) is in fact a collagen of human remains with a chronological span of some 20,000 years, and can therefore not be taken as samples indicating the DNA sequences of early modern humans at 25 ka BP (Zilhão, 2006a). The dating of the examined aDNA material has large implications for the estimated potential Neandertal mtDNA contribution above. However, it has to be remembered that the examination of aDNA is connected with several uncertainties, not being specifically retrieved for genetic analyses it is often of unsatisfactory quality (O'Rourke *et al*, 2000). Combined with the early H. sapiens mandible from Pestera cu Oase (Trinkhaus *et al*, 2003), indicating that the time of admixture might have been as early as 40 ka BP, implies that the level of possible admixture proposed by Serre *et al* (2004) might be substantially underestimated (Zilhão, 2006a). In fact, it has been shown by Cooper *et al* (2004) that Neandertal genetic contribution could be anywhere between 1% and 53% based on the genetic evidence alone.

A recent study undertaken by Currat & Excoffier (2004), attempts to combine the genetic evidence with the archaeological record from this time period. By subdividing Europe into small isolated territories, assuming that each territory harboured one H. sapiens and one Neandertal deme, they propose a scenario where H. sapiens colonised Europe one territory after another. Due to inter-specific competition, Neandertal populations subsequently became extinct. By subdividing them into isolated territories, suggesting no consequences outside these territories, they conclude that "even for very few admixture events, the contribution of the Neandertal lineages in the current gene pool should be very large" (Currat & Excoffier, 2004:2265).

However, several of the criteria they use in their analysis are questionable. First, the archaeological record does not support the assumption that H. sapiens possessed considerable competitive advantages to Neandertals (further discussed in chapter 6). Second, a scenario where one population (or more accurately; one population deme) completely replaces an entire continental population, one territory at a time, virtually without any genetic exchange, would be ethnographically unique. Instead, Zilhão (2006a) argues that the presence of exogamic marital exchange, seen among interacting hunter-gatherer groups, would be more plausible. Females carrying Neandertal mtDNA can only be expected to become dominant if Europe is considered a genetically isolated territory. The empirical record shows that hunter-gatherer groups engaging in exogamic marital networks would have to maintain alliances across thousands of square kilometres (Wobst, 1974). Under such conditions, genetic drift would be a substantial factor regarding Neandertal mtDNA persistence. This point is further strengthened by the fact that the available genetic evidence shows that there was a general loss of Pleistocene genetic lineages. In fact, none of the H. sapiens lineages examined by Serre *et al* (2004) are probable contributors to extant human DNA (Zilhão, 2006a).

Furthermore, contamination from present day DNA material is a considerable source of error (Cooper & Poinar, 2000). The exclusively non-Neandertal aDNA extracted from early H. sapiens may therefore just as well be a case of post-excavation contamination. In fact, studies show that human DNA can potentially be extracted from all fossil remains:

> *"In fact, because human DNA sequences can readily be retrieved from ancient animal remains, we believe that many published studies that report ancient human DNA sequences are unreliable"* (Hofreiter *et al*, 2001:354).

The risk of contamination represents further bias in that modern human DNA found in a Neandertal specimen would immediately be identified as contamination, but modern human DNA found in early H. sapiens specimens would be virtually undetectable. As a result, aDNA studies of early H. sapiens seemingly not containing any traces of Neandertal mtDNA might simply be a case of extracting entirely contaminated modern DNA. Experiment trying to decontaminate contaminated DNA material, show that it is virtually impossible, even when the most extreme decontamination methods are applied (Cooper & Poinar, 2000).

As seen above, all the methodological problems notwithstanding, a large amount of evidence indicate that Neandertals did not contribute to the present day gene pool. One important point to be made here is that this does not necessarily have any implications for the nature of the extinction of Neandertals, as argued by proponents of the RAO model. No traces of

Neandertal DNA in extant populations do not *a priory* rule out the possibility for major Neandertal contribution to the gene pool of early H. sapiens migrating into Europe. The same is the case when examining contemporary Neandertals and H. sapiens, because one can not be sure of not simply examining one of early H. sapiens which do not carry any Neandertal DNA, as opposed to other contemporaries who did. Therefore, examining the DNA lineages immediately after the proposed mixing event would be preferable. This raises two problems: 1. The relatively few human remains from this period and the generally poor quality of the DNA material which these produce. 2. The reliance of incorporating the actual nature of the social networks necessary for substantial interbreeding to take place.

Point nr. 2 is perhaps of special importance because, as shown by Zilhão (2006a), the chosen scenario of the proposed admixture would have large implications for the results of any DNA analysis estimating the maximum Neandertal DNA contribution possible without being detectable in extant DNA lineages. Therefore, when conducting such an analysis, archaeological arguments can not be ignored. In fact, DNA analysis trying to examine Neandertal DNA contribution without incorporating archaeological argument would be virtually valueless. The following chapter will examine the archaeological record and its implications for the nature of Neandertal/H. sapiens contact and the subsequent demise of Neandertals.

Chapter 6

Neandertal extinction as a result of competitive disadvantage?

> *"But from the view-point of the archaeological evidence there seems little doubt that the first exponents of upper palaeolithic technology in southwestern France were of essentially local, as opposed to exotic, origin." (Mellars, 1973:273).*

As seen in the preceding chapter, the nature of the demise of the Neandertals cannot be resolved using genetic and fossil analysis alone. A relatively quick replacement with little or no genetic admixture between Neandertals and H. sapiens would be inconceivable without the intruding H. sapiens having a massive competitive advantage. Numerous competitive advantages have been proposed, both behavioural superiority and cognitive advantages due to biological differences. This chapter will discuss what information the archaeological record from the Middle- to Upper Paleolithic transition can provide regarding the behavioural, and by extension cognitive aspects of the demise of the Neandertals.

The period from 40 000 to 35 000 years ago is one of the most distinct in human prehistory (Mellars, 1994). This relatively short period constitutes the dispersal of Aurignacian tool-makers across Eurasia and the subsequent almost complete disappearance of the Neandertals from the archaeological record. Major shifts in the empirical record in the Eurasian areas takes place, the archaeological record changes more than it has for the previous one million years (Klein, 1999a, 1999b, Bar-Yosef, 1993). These changes marked the transition from the Middle Palaeolithic to the Upper Palaeolithic period, and have by some scholars been dubbed the "Upper Palaeolithic Revolution" (Bar-Yosef, 2002).

The abrupt nature of the Middle- to Upper Palaeolithic transition has led many scholars to conclude that it was due to a complete population replacement. As reviewed in preceding chapters, this view is to some degree supported by the fossil evidence, as it roughly corresponds with the disappearance of the Neandertals (Bordes, 1971). However, an expansion of the available empirical data, both in Eurasia and in other regions of the world has provided new life to the discussion. Many scholars now question whether or not the transition was as abrupt as previously perceived (McBrearty & Brooks, 2000, Deacon, 1998,

Henshilwood & d'Errico, 2005), whether or not the theoretical framework from which the empirical record has been interpreted is acceptable (Henshilwood & Marean, 2003, Speth, 2004, d'Errico, 2003), and whether or not the fossil record and DNA analysis really does reveal a correspondence between the demise of the Neandertals and the transition to the Upper Palaeolithic (d'Errico, 2003, Wolpoff *et al*, 2004, Zilhão, 2006a,d).

Fossil evidence

As mentioned earlier (chapter 5), there is no justification for exclusively ascribing any of the earliest Upper Palaeolithic technocomplexes to either Neandertals or H. sapiens. The strongest indication for direct Neandertal and H. sapiens contact is the time span from when H. sapiens first entered Eurasia until the last Neandertals vanish from the archaeological record. If it can be established that Neandertals and H. sapiens coexisted on a regional scale over a long period of time this would make it highly unlikely that no interaction occurred. Considering only the fossil evidence for illuminating the period of overlap is arguably the most secure method of establishing the actual length of it. The problem however, lies in the scarcity of fossils dating to this period (d'Errico *et al* 1998), and the problem of reliability of radiocarbon dating during this time period (Hughen *et al 2004*).

Early Upper Palaeolithic H. sapiens

> *"As stressed by other authors (…), it can hardly be regarded as pure coincidence that the rapid development of Upper Paleolithic industries in Europe occurs nearly simultaneously with a biological revolution marked by the arrival of anatomically modern humans. Overwhelming paleontological evidence supports that, in Europe, Neanderthals were responsible for the Mousterian; and while human remains associated with Aurignacian layers are rare, it is generally assumed that early modern humans were responsible for the Aurignacian." (Hublin & Bailey 2005:105)*

H. sapiens fossils dating to the crucial period of the early Upper Palaeolithic are relatively few, and recent developments within dating methods have questioned the initial dating of many specimens. Some of these specimens also display physical features which deviate from fully modern humans (Trinkhaus 2005). The only directly dated H. sapiens remains dated to the early Aurignacian period are the remains from Peştera cu Oase, Peştera Muierii, Peştera Cioclovina in Romania, Kent's Cavern, England and Mladeč in the Czech Republic (Wild *et al* 2005), Vogelherd, Germany The Oase 1 and Oase 2 seem to be roughly contemporaneous, dating to ≈40.5 cal BP (Rougier *et al* 2007, Trinkhaus *et al* 2003). The Peștera Muierii and Peștera Cioclovina remains are dated to ~30 ^{14}C ka BP and ~29 ^{14}C ka BP, respectively. Kent's Cavern in England was dated at ~31 ^{14}C ka BP. The Mladeč fossil remains have recently been re-dated using accelerator mass spectrometry (AMS) radiocarbon dating, resulting in an uncalibrated age of 31 ^{14}C ka BP (Wild *et al* 2005), placing these human remains within the time period of the initial Upper Palaeolithic.

With the exception of the Mladeč remains, none of the above early Upper Palaeolithic H. sapiens remains are found in direct association with the Aurignacian technocomplex, and the stratigraphic context of the Mladeč remains has been seriously contested (Svoboda 2000). There is also a lively ongoing debate regarding the actual modernity of the human remains found at this site. Some authors argue that these remains, although displaying some archaic features, should be characterized as anatomically modern (Klein 1999a, Serre *et al* 2004). In recent years however, this view has been challenged by several authors (Zilhão, 2006b). Based on a pairwise difference analysis of Mladeč craniums (Mladeč 5 and 6) and early H. sapiens remains from Qafzeh and Skhul in Israel, Wolpoff *et al.* (2001) found that the human remains from Mladeč displayed a similar number of morphological differences with the H. sapiens remains (14.0 for Mladeč 1, and 11.6 for Mladeč 2) as with a number of Neandertal specimens (14.8 for Mladeč 1 and 7.8 for Mladeč 2) from across Europe. Thus, it was argued that the Mladeč cranial remains could not be "grouped with the Levantines to the exclusion of European Neandertals." (Wolpoff *et al* 2001:296). Although this pairwise difference analysis has been rejected on grounds of a speculative selection of specimens included in the analysis (Bräuer *et al* 2004), it nevertheless illustrates the difficulty of dichotomizing between intra- and inter specific variability and even sexual dimorphism. This problem has also been raised regarding the Oase 2 Cranium (Rougier *et al* 2007). Combined with recent redating of other presumed Early Upper Palaeolithic H. sapiens sites like Velika Pećina, Croatia (≈5 ka BP (Smith *et al* 1999)), Zlatý kůň, Czech Republic, 12.9 ka BP (Svoboda *et al* 2002), Vogelherd, Germany, 3.9-5 ^{14}C ka BP (Conrad *et al* 2004), Cro-Magnon, France, 27.8 ^{14}C ka BP (Conrad *et al* 2004), Prokop's Cave, 5-6 ka BP (Svoboda 2005) and Hahnöfersand, 7.5 ka BP (Terberger *et al* 2001) the empirical record directly connecting the H. sapiens to the early Aurignacian is virtually non-existent.

Although "overwhelming evidence" (Hublin & Bailey 2005:105) supports the association between the Aurignacian technocomplex and H. sapiens, there is currently virtually no evidence supporting the widespread *a priory* assumption that the presence of early Aurignacian tool-kits can be taken as evidence for H. sapiens occupation. In fact, the recent revised dates of H. sapiens fossils "has removed any clear association of diagnostic human remains with the Aurignacian before ≈34,000 BP." (Higham *et al* 2006).

Neandertal occupation across Europe during the time of transition
Neandertal fossil evidence dating within the crucial time period of the Middle- to Upper Paleolithic transition is abundant. However, nowhere in Europe do Neandertal remains, or Neandertal associated cultural manifestations postdate 41 ka BP, except south of the Ebro Basin (Zilhão, 2006b). Two possible exceptions from this distribution pattern are the Vindija remains, Croatia and the Mezmaiskaya Neandertal infant, northern Caucasus (Golovanova *et al*, 1999, Ovchinnikov *et al*, 2000). New dating methods, and in particular improvement in sample pretreatment techniques for radiocarbon dating bone (Higham *et al*, 2006), has recently changed the chronology of the two Neandertal specimens from the G_1 level at Vindija, Croatia. They were initially dated to ≈28-29 ka BP (Smith *et al*, 1999), but have recently been redated to approximately ≈32-33 ka BP, or perhaps even older (Higham *et al*, 2006). The Mezmaiskaya remains has been dated to ca. 29 ka ^{14}C BP (Ovchinnikov *et al*, 2000), but the validity of such a recent date has been contested, and they are now considered to be contaminated by modern carbon. Dating of the Mousterian level associated with the fossil remains suggests an age of ~40 ka BP (Skinner *et al*, 2005).

South of the Ebro River, southern Iberia, several Neandertal sites postdate 30 ka BP. At Zafarraya, southern Spain the Mousterian toolmakers may have lasted to ca. 27 ka BP (Tattersall & Schwartz, 1999). These late dates for the Mousterian at Zafarraya have now been dismissed by some scholars (Finlayson *et al*, 2006, Mellars, 2006a), based on new dates presented by Michel *et al* (2003). However, the original dates published by Hublin *et al* (1995) cannot be completely dismissed based exclusively on the new available dates because the dates ranging from 5 ka BP to 140 ka. BP may be explained by a high probability of interstratigraphic mobility in the area of the site from which these dates were obtained (Hublin & Bailey, 2005). Another site which has produced evidence of late Mousterian occurrences is Figueira Brava in Portugal. In addition to a tool industry described as "Typical Mousterian, rich in denticulates, with non-Levallois debitage and a non-Levalloisian facies"

(Raposo, 2000:99), this site has also produced a Neandertal upper premolar. *Patella sp.* shells associated with Mousterian tools have been dated to ≈31 ka BP, indicating a late occupation by Neandertals (Zilhão, 2000).

The youngest dates of Mousterian levels come from Gorham's Cave, Gibraltar. The presence of Neandertals in Gibraltar has been known ever since the Neandertal cranium from Forbe's Quarry, recovered in 1848, was classified as Neandertal in 1864 by Hugh Falconer (Trinkhaus & Shipman, 1992). The Middle- to Upper Paleolithic transition was dated to ~32.3 ka BP, obtained by AMS dating on charcoal (Barton *et al*, 1999). New excavations at this cave from 1999 to 2005 provided new dates for the uppermost Mousterian. The new dates suggest that the site was repeatedly occupied by Mousterian toolmakers over a period of ca. 10 000 years, until 28 ka BP, and possibly as early as 24 ka BP (Finlayson *et al*, 2006). The youngest dates, at 24 ka BP should be treated with caution because during the most recent excavations there where six cases (Sample no. 9-14) where a stratigraphic layer was older than the underlying level (Finlayson *et al*, 2006:852).

The overall picture of the Iberian Peninsula south of the Ebro Basin shows a biocultural sequence which is very distinct from the rest of Europe. The Mousterian survives until 28 ka BP, maybe even longer. The Neandertals from southern Iberia do not seem to have developed a transitional technocomplex of their own. A fully Mousterian tool-type technology is displayed in association even with the very latest known Neandertals, as seen in Gorham's Cave (Barton *et al*, 1999). The archaeological record shows no evidence of transitional technocomplexes; the Upper Paleolithic has an abrupt appearance, thus favouring a total replacement scenario in these areas.

Interaction

The chronological overlap between Neandertals and H. sapiens has been known ever since the revised chronology of the Mount Carmel remains were published (Bar-Yosef *et al*, 1986, Lewin, 1988, Valladas *et al*, 1988). Whether or not there was any direct or indirect contact between the two species however, is a lot more complicated to determine. Although dating methods are constantly refined (Mellars, 2006a), no dating method of the resolution needed to unequivocally establish evidence for contemporaniety on a local scale is presently available. As reviewed above, Aurignacian assemblages directly associated with H. sapiens fossil remains are much less abundant than Neandertal remains directly associated with Mousterian sites (Hublin & Bailey, 2005). Interstratigraphic Mousterian and Aurignacian sites are also rare, and therefore make it hard to actually connect the two hominid species in chronological overlap in the same geographical area, and even interstratigraphic sequences will not positively prove the contemporaniety of Neandertals and H. sapiens. In fact, it only indicates a sequence where the two species occupied the site at *different* times in an overlapping chronology.

Competition

The view of Neandertals becoming extinct as a result of competitive disadvantages has been favoured among scientists for a long time. However, to determine whether or not Neandertals and H. sapiens were in direct competition with one another is difficult. According to Clive Finlayson, competition would only be evident if two populations utilize similar resources to an extent of reaching "carrying capacity" for that region (2004:153). Based on the available paleoenvironmental data, he argues that the Neandertal and H. sapiens populations did not reach maximum carrying capacity in Europe during the Middle- to Upper Paleolithic transition, and that this would indicate that competition was not a driving force behind the demise of Neandertals (Finlayson, 2004). However, competition between hominid groups can arguably be based on other factors than ecology. Cultural aspects, like for example ideology, can also result in a competitive situation. Ian Hodder has shown that populations engaging in competition tend to increase their expressions of social identity (Hodder, 1979). Therefore, the intensification of symbolic expressions, characterising the onset of the Upper Paleolithic, may partially be explained by the increased need for social identification due to a competitive situation. This would also be supported by the fact that within populations living south of the Ebro River, who never interacted with migrating H. sapiens (Finlayson & Giles Pacheco, 2000, Zilhão, 2000), Middle Palaeolithic technology persisted long after the appearance of the Upper Paleolithic in the rest of Eurasia (Barton *et al*, 1999, Zilhão, 2006b).

Technology

Advocates of the RAO model argues that the appearance of the so-called Mode 4 technology (Fig. 6.1) (Foley & Lahr, 1997) was linked to the development of anatomically modern humans. Various degrees of connection between biology and culture are postulated. In its strongest form, anatomical evolution would be expected to directly coincide with the development of Mode 4 technology. However, the archaeological record reveals discrepancies between anatomical evolution and cultural development. An increasing empirical record is showing anatomically modern humans associated with Mode 4 technological traits prior to the Upper Palaeolithic (Singer & Wymer, 1982, Brooks *et al*, 1995, Yellen *et al*, 1995, Henshilwood & Sealy, 1997, McBrearty & Brooks, 2000, Henshilwood *et al* 2001). To some degree this may be viewed as consistent with the RAO model because it may indicate early development of "modern" behaviour within the evolution of anatomical modernity. However, accepting that Mode 4 technologies at least partially developed in Africa long before the initial dispersal across Eurasia, not only create a problem in ascribing these abilities as the driving force for the initial dispersal out of Africa, it also creates a problem in explaining the absence of such traits in cultures contemporary to Upper Palaeolithic Eurasia. If behavioural traits consistent with Mode 4 technology did in fact develop within Africa prior to the initial dispersal across the Old World, one would expect that subsequent H. Sapiens all over the world would share these traits. The clear evidence of H. sapiens associated with Mousterian (Mode 3) technology in the Middle East (Skhul and Qafzeh) is not consistent with this assumption. Furthermore, the fact that relatively "modern" technocomplexes, like "Howieson Poort" in South Africa, are subsequently replaced by typically Mode 3 technologies (Foley & Lahr, 1997), in addition to blade technology appearing and disappearing within the Middle Paleolithic in Europe (Soressi, 2005), shows that no simple correlation between anatomical evolution and technological advancement can be established.

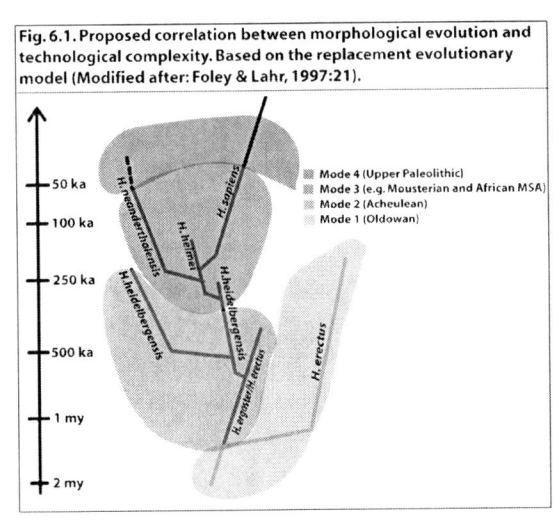

Fig. 6.1. Proposed correlation between morphological evolution and technological complexity. Based on the replacement evolutionary model (Modified after: Foley & Lahr, 1997:21).

Transitional industries

The identification of so-called "transitional" technocomplexes (containing both Mode 3 and Mode 4 technology) discredited the view of the Upper Palaeolithic transition being extremely abrupt. Features like end scrapers, burins, bifacially worked foliates, bone tools and personal ornaments (d'Errico *et al* 1998, Zilhão & d'Errico, 1999), as well as Mousterian features like side scrapers and denticulates, characterises the transitional industries as Mousterian derived Upper Palaeolithic industries. The best known transitional industries in Europe are the Châtelperronian (Hublin *et al* 1995, d'Errico 2003, d'Errico *et al* 1998), Uluzzian (Koumouzelis *et al* 2001,) and the Szeletian (Allsworth-Jones 1986). Hominid remains from levels displaying transitional industries are few (Churchill & Smith 2000), and identifying the actual manufacturers of these industries has therefore been difficult.

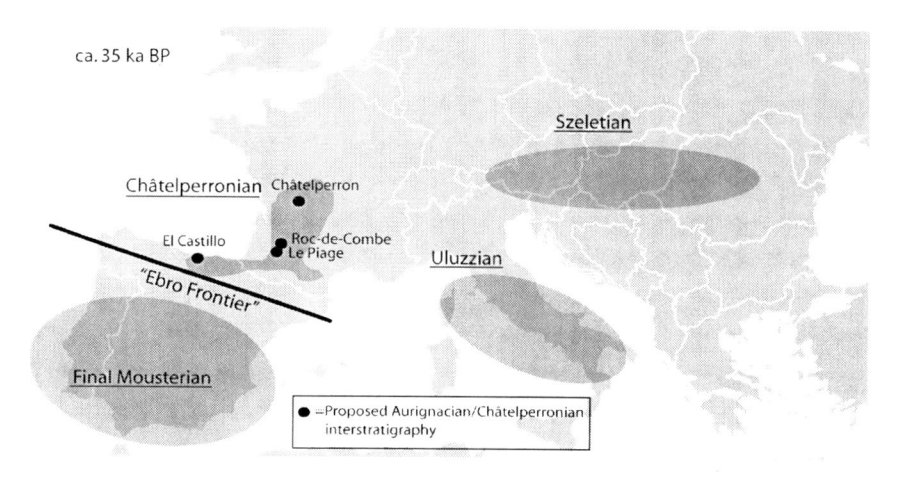

Fig. 6.2. Distribution map of the Châtelperronian, Uluzzian and Szeletian and the "Ebro Frontier" (after: Raposo, 2000, Zilhão, 2000)

In 1979 a fragmented Neandertal was found in association with Châtelperronian tools at Saint-Césaire, south-western France (Harrold, 2000). The Châtelperronian industry had been thought to have been made by H. sapiens ever since Otto Hauser and colleagues excavated an H. sapiens grave immediately above the Mousterian level at Combe Chapelle in 1909, which probably was intrusive of an overlying Aurignacian level (Gambier 1989). Neandertal remains in a Châtelperronian level was explained in very different ways. Some authors, favouring the RAO model, saw the Saint-Cèsaire find as a natural effect of the contemporaniety between Neandertals and H. sapiens, a case of Neandertal acculturation (Stringer *et al.* 1984). Others stressed that only one identified Neandertal with Châtelperronian tools were not enough to positively classify the Châtelperronian as a Neandertal industry (Morin *et al*, 2005). Scholars favouring the hypothesis that Neandertals were the direct ancestors of modern humans, argued that the Châtelperronian manufacturing

Neandertal were direct evidence of Neandertals evolving into H. sapiens (Wolpoff 1981). The association between Neandertals and the Châtelperronian were further strengthened by the classification of a temporal bone from Grotte du Renne, Arcy-sur-Cure in France, as Neandertal (Hublin *et al* 1996).

As for the Uluzzian and Szeletian, very few associated hominid remains have been recovered. At Grotta del Cavallo, Italy, two human milk teeth were found in Uluzzian level E. These teeth were originally classified as H. sapiens, but later re-evaluation of the teeth has concluded that they are morphologically closer to Neandertals, although they can not be positively ascribed to either of the two (Churchill & Smith 2000). Two Szeletian sites have produced human fossil evidence. At the Upper Remete Cave, Hungary, three heavily worn teeth thought to have belonged to a single Neandertal were recovered. However, as with the human teeth from Grotta del Cavallo, they cannot unequivocally be classified as Neandertal. This is also the case for a tooth recovered at Dzeravá Skála in Slovakia, making the overall association between hominid remains and the Uluzzian and Szeletian inconclusive. Notwithstanding, the clear association between Neandertals and the Châtelperronian industry shows that some Neandertal populations undoubtedly possessed the *capability* of producing tool-kits containing Mode 4 technologies. Phylogenetic evidence can also be sought through the nature of the Châtelperronian, Uluzzian and Szeletian assemblages themselves. If these transitional industries shows evidence of being locally evolved from the preceding Middle Palaeolithic industries, it would also strongly support the view that these industries were manufactured by Neandertals.

The Aurignacian and transitional technocomplexes compared

Detailed reconstruction of core reduction and flintknapping from the Châtelperronian levels at Roc de Combe and La-Côte showed that the Châtelperronian industry is very distinct from the Aurignacian and shows clear association with regional Mousterian of Acheulian Tradition (Harrold, 2000). In fact, François Bordes argued as early as in 1954 that technological features of the Châtelperronian, like the Châtelperron points, side-scrapers and denticulates show clear association with the preceding Mousterian industries of the same region (Mellars, 1996). This is clearly demonstrated by the morphology of the Châtelperron point, described as *"nothing more than a Mousterian backed knife translated into a blade technology"* (Mellars, 1973:273). The local origin of the Châtelperronian industry is also supported by its geographically restricted occurrence, making an origin outside this area improbable (Mellars,

1999). In fact, the evidence of cultural continuity from the Mousterian of Acheulian tradition to the Châtelperronian was initially described by Mellars as "*virtually conclusive*" (1973:273). Which kind of raw material preferred seems to be fundamentally different between the Aurignacian and the Châtelperronian technocomplexes. Châtelperronian sites produce three and a half time as many tools made on ivory relative to Aurignacian sites. Furthermore, reindeer antler which were used in the Aurignacian is absent in the Châtelperronian (d'Errico et al, 1998).

The Szeletian, characterized by "the technique of flat, bifacial retouch" (Leaf-points) (Svoboda & Simán, 1989), most probably evolved from local Micoquian (Middle Paleolithic) industries, thus providing indirect evidence for the Szeletian industry being manufactured by Neandertals (Allsworth-Jones, 1986, Svoboda, 2005, Kozlowski, 2004), although some have characterized the Szeletian as a locally adaptive variation of the Aurignacian (Smith, 1982). As for the Uluzzian of Italy, it is characterized by "crescent-shaped backed pieces, or lunates, as well as end scrapers, side scrapers and burins, and bone points or *sagaies*" (Churchill & Smith, 2000:76), and it has been characterized as a regional variant of the Châtelperronian (Gioia, 1990, in: d'Errico & Sánchez Goñi 2003[1])

Acculturation or innovation
There is currently a widespread consensus regarding Neandertals producing, or at least possessing Upper Paleolithic (Mode 4) technology. However, the association between Neandertals and Mode 4 technology has been explained in different ways. Two main views can be summarized as follows:

1. Acquisition of Upper Paleolithic technological features through acculturation, trade or collecting from abandoned H. sapiens sites (ApSimon, 1980, Stringer & Gamble, 1993, Stringer & Grün, 1991, Stringer et al, 1984, Hublin et al, 1996, Harrold, 1989, Mellars, 1973, Wynn & Coolidge, 2004).
2. Neandertals developed their own Upper Paleolithic assemblages. This view is held by some proponents of the subsequent population replacement across Eurasia (d'Errico, 2003, d'Errico & Nowell, 2000, d'Errico et al, 1998, Zilhão & d'Errico, 1999), called the "Multiple Species Model" (d'Errico, 2003), and by proponents of

---
[1] Original paper not available to me

Multiregional evolution (Brose & Wolpoff, 1971, Wolpoff, 1981, 2004, Wolpoff & Frayer, 1992, Wolpoff *et al*, 2001).

The acculturation hypothesis is based on the notion that Neandertals did not possess the cognitive capabilities necessary for independently developing Upper Paleolithic technology (Mithen, 1996). It also rests on the Neandertals being behaviourally inferior to the H. sapiens, hence trying to adapt to their way of life. This explanation model was first formulated by Richard Klein;

"For the moment the possible significance of so-called transitional cultures is a matter for open speculation. An interpretation (speculation) which is at least as plausible as the missing-link hypothesis is that the transitional cultures reflect diffusion of Upper Paleolithic traits into a Mousterian context. This interpretation can be illustrated with facts on the French "transitional culture", the Périgordian I or Châtelperronian." (Klein, 1973:115).

Numerous cognitive and behavioural capacities have been suggested to be lacking in the Neandertal population. The capacity for producing art (Mithen, 1996), complex communicational systems (Mellars, 2004), organized social structures (Bar-Yosef, 2000), production of bone tools (Mellars, 1973) blade technology (Klein, 1973), personal ornaments and specialized hunting (Mellars, 2003) is some of the traits proposed (Fig.3.1). The acculturation model is dependant on a chronological framework showing that the above mentioned technologies first appeared within H. sapiens populations, and subsequently spread to Neandertal populations. Illuminating potential cultural contact between the two populations through chronological overlap is therefore vital for this hypothesis to sustain plausible; *"some degree of contact, interaction, and transfer of technology would be not only plausible but totally predictable"* (Mellars, 1999:348). Furthermore, the common description of the Middle Paleolithic technocomplexes as archaic and non-progressive during the entire sequence, as opposed to the progressive nature of the technocomplexes appearing broadly simultaneously with the expansion of H. sapiens across Eurasia, is described as highly unlikely to be a coincidence (Mellars, 1999, 2005).

Proponents of the view that Neandertals themselves are the inventive force behind the Early Upper Paleolithic (transitional) industries criticise the acculturation hypothesis on several grounds. The differentiated use of the term "acculturation" represents one of the main criticisms:

"The first problem with the imitation model is that of the meaning of "acculturation," a concept for which no consensus exists in cultural anthropology (...). The term "acculturation" is usually associated with asymmetrical relationships of dominating and dominated- of colonisers who inevitably overwhelm and assimilate the colonised because of their inherent superiority (...)." (d'Errico *et al*, 1998:S3).

Central in this view is the emphasis on regional continuity in the Neandertal stone tool assemblages. Contrary to proponents of acculturation, these authors advocate that the Middle Paleolithic record in Eurasia show clear evidence of behavioural traits which can be considered "modern". Specialised hunting (Chase, 1986, Grayson & Delpech, 2002), blade production (Soressi, 2005), wooden tools (Thieme, 1997), burial of the dead (Riel-Salvatore & Clark, 2001) and symbolic expressions (Zilhão, 2007) are some of the traits visible in the Eurasian archaeological record prior to the Upper Paleolithic. The presence of these traits is proposed as evidence for Neandertals possessing the cognitive capabilities necessary for independently producing the transitional industries (Soressi, 2005). Combined with the evidence of the *in situ* development of the transitional industries, they conclude that Neandertals independently developed Upper Paleolithic technology, different of that produced by H. sapiens (d'Errico *et al*, 1998, d'Errico, 2003).

Chronology
Although the empirical data strongly supports the view of the Châtelperronian being produced by local Neandertals, and subsequently strengthening the indicative evidence of the same conclusion regarding the other transitional industries in Eurasia, it does not exclude the possibility of acculturation. The blade technologies of these industries were made by essentially Middle Paleolithic reduction sequences. However, this may be explained by the imitation of an intrusive end product by applying locally derived reduction sequences. The most important data for examining the question of acculturation is therefore chronological.

The general stratigraphic pattern across south-western Europe shows that the Châtelperronian levels underlie the Aurignacian, documented by thirty occurrences across the Châtelperronian distribution area (Zilhão & d'Errico, 1999). Three occurrences of interstratifications seem to be in direct contradiction to this overall pattern, Le Piage and Roc-de-Combe, France and El Pendo, Spain (Mellars, 1999). Re-evaluation of these three sites has led several authors to conclude that none of them can unambiguously be attributed to chronological overlap between Aurignacian and Châtelperronian populations (d'Errico et al, 1998, Kozlowski, 2004, Zilhão, 2006d). Another occurrence of interstratification has recently been proposed at Châtelperron in central France (Gravina et al, 2005). This interpretation was subsequently criticised because of severe stratigraphic disturbance on the site (Zilhão et al, 2006). The implications of the possible interstratification at Châtelperron is currently being discussed (Mellars et al, 2007), and more data is clearly needed to establish whether or not there were a chronological overlap between the Châtelperronian and Aurignacian in southwestern Europe. However, overall the stratigraphic record shows an unquestionable pattern of the Châtelperronian preceding the Aurignacian across southwestern Europe, and even though some occurrence of interstratification are accepted, this does not preclude the possibility of Mode 4 technology first appearing in Neandertal populations. It has also been argued by Wolpoff and colleagues that even though acculturation is accepted as the explanation for the transitional industries, "one does not copy what one cannot understand" (Wolpoff et al, 2004:538).

Stratigraphic sequences containing both Châtelperronian and Aurignacian assemblages are very few. Radiometric dates can therefore be a useful tool to attribute to the stratigraphic data. In south-western Europe several sites from Northern Spain have produced dates which do not concur with the general stratigraphic pattern from this region. However, most of these sites display stratigraphic inconsistencies (for detailed discussion see Zilhão, 2006d). At El Castillo, the Aurignacian levels have produced very early dates, from 41,6 to ca. 45 ka BP. The Aurignacian at this site has been divided into three sub-levels, B1, B2 and C. The dates were obtained from an area of the site which has not produced any diagnostic Aurignacian artefacts. Attributing the dates to "Aurignacian" chronology was based on the assumed stratigraphic correlation to a previously proposed Aurignacian level from another part of the cave. Re-excavation of El Castillo showed that the level previously designated as "Aurignacian" were in fact a one meter thick palimpsest containing both Aurignacian and Mousterian components (Zilhão & d'Errico, 1999, Zilhão, 2006d). A similar situation has been claimed for the early dates of Geißenklösterle (Zilhão & d'Errico, 1999), but this interpretation has subsequently been rejected by Teyssandier et al. (2006) based on new taphonomic evaluation, refittings, geoarchaeological and micro-morphological analyses and comparison of lithic and organic productions. Geißenklösterle notwithstanding, the case of El Castillo clearly reveals the problems related to many of the sites central in the Middle- to Upper Paleolithic transition which were excavated during times when the excavation criteria was vastly different from today. Re-analysis of a large part of the previously excavated material is therefore clearly needed in order to verify or redefining the original conclusions made by the excavators.

Outside southwestern Europe, there is also a general pattern of the Aurignacian post-dating the earliest Upper Paleolithic technocomplexes (Svoboda et al, 1996, Kuhn et al, 2004b). In fact, in Eastern Europe (Meignen et al, 2004), Caucasia (Meshveliani et al, 2004) and central and north-eastern Asia (Otte, 2004), the Aurignacian is poorly represented and sometimes not represented at all. As for the areas where the Aurignacian is present, like Central Europe (Kozlowski, 2004, Svoboda & Simán, 1989), Crimea (Marks & Monigal, 2004) and the Levant (Kuhn et al, 2004a), it clearly postdates the earliest Upper Paleolithic assemblages. Although exceptions based on radiometric dates do occur, as for example Geißenklösterle and Willendorf II (Teyssandier et al, 2006), the overall empirical record supports this general stratigraphic sequence.

Conclusion
Hitherto the empirical record arguably does not support the wide-spread view of the Aurignacian being the cultural bearer of behavioural "modernity". To the contrary, the stratigraphic pattern by and large supports the view that the initial Upper Paleolithic is best represented by the transitional industries. Considering the uncertainties of radiometric dating within this time-range, stratigraphic reconstruction is currently the best tool for establishing a chronological framework showing the relative chronology between transitional industries and the Aurignacian. Further detailed elaboration is clearly needed to evaluate whether or not the discrepancies between the stratigraphic and radiometric evidence is a result of biased methodology or if it represent valid information on inter-location chronology.

On a theoretical basis, the acculturation view can be criticised on several grounds. As mentioned above, the supposed situation of interaction, with Neandertals as a passive receiver of cultural traits is also based on an *a priori* assumption that (1) Neandertals were cognitively unable to produce these objects themselves and (2) were behaviourally inferior to H. sapiens and would therefore have advantage of adapting to H. sapiens behaviour. Both these assumptions are based largely on negative evidence, and are to some degree in direct contradiction to the empirical record. The apparent lack of certain behavioural traits can be explained in numerous ways; population density, benign climatic and ecological conditions, depositional discrepancies, lack of cognitive capabilities, biased taphonomic conditions or simply the lack of knowledge of *how* to behave in certain ways. Notwithstanding, the lack of certain modern behavioural traits in the Middle Paleolithic, have traditionally automatically been ascribed to the lack of cognitive capability. Applying the same criteria when examining several human groups from the ethnographic present would inevitably deprive them of the capability for "modern human behaviour", a conclusion which is unquestionably faulty (Speth, 2004).

There is no theoretical foundation for an uncritical connection between behaviour and cognition. Such a universal connection would only be valid if all people at all times sought maximum subsistence exploitation, and all people lived within comparable climatic and ecological conditions. In such a scenario, people's success in obtaining optimal foraging strategies would provide a litmus-test of behavioural capabilities, and by extension cognitive capabilities. However, this would be a gross simplification of both the present and the past (Henshilwood & Marean, 2003, Speth, 2004). Identifying *how* people behaved is not the same as identifying their behavioural *capacity*. Illuminating behavioural traits of past population should therefore not be considered the final goal, but the first step in understanding their range of cognitive capabilities. Several authors have stressed that the Aurignacian represents only one of potentially numerous variation of behavioural "modernity" (e.g. Foley & Lahr, 1997, McBrearty & Brooks, 2000, Henshilwood, 2004).

How we perceive "reality" is inflicted by the names we chose to give different aspects of it. Taxonomic categorisation can therefore be an important factor in scientific research. This is perhaps especially true when dealing with the Middle- to Upper Paleolithic transition. When the transitional industries were first identified there was a widespread consensus of the Upper Paleolithic appearing abrupt. The clear cut dichotomising between the Middle Paleolithic Mousterian and the Upper Paleolithic Aurignacian fit perfectly into this picture, but the transitional industries did not. Giving the so-called transitional industries independent names, underlines the distinctiveness of these industries and maintains the picture of the Mousterian as a static, non-progressive technocomplex. Choosing a different approach, viewing the transitional industries as highly developed Mousterian assemblages (which would be supported by the evidence of *in situ* development of these industries), would have large implication on our view on both the Mousterian, Neandertals and the Middle- to Upper Paleolithic transition.

Neandertal extinction as a result of competitive disadvantages has long been the favoured hypothesis. More detailed analysis, both within the Middle Paleolithic, transitional, and fully Upper Paleolithic industries has produced an empirical record far more complex and mosaic than previously assumed. Middle Paleolithic Neandertals displayed the capacity for producing blade technology (Soressi, 2005), symbolic expressions (Zilhão, 2007), specialized hunting (Gaudzinski & Roebroeks, 2000) and burial of the dead. Accepting the accumulating evidence of Neandertals being the manufactures of all the transitional industries across Eurasia would dramatically increase the Neandertal capability for behavioural traits previously assumed to be confined to H. sapiens populations. Thus, the empirical record can no longer be seen as the manifestation of one behaviourally inferior population being replaced by a behaviourally superior population. It rather suggests a mosaic of behaviourally different, but equally "modern" populations applying different solutions to similar challenges. The debate regarding the demise of the Neandertals has to long been characterised as a comparative analysis of intelligence. It would be more productive to place the emphasis on intra-specific research, both morphologically and behaviourally, to illuminate why Neandertals became unable to maintain their population density and eventually succumbed. The first step towards such an approach would be accepting Neandertals as a distinct population solving new challenges on their own premises.

Chapter 7

Climatic conditions as a source for extinction?

Was climate one of the factors leading to the demise of Neandertals? Many different scenarios involving climatic influence on the demographic development and subsequent demise of Neandertals during OIS-3 has been proposed. Due to uncertainties in the dating methods, paleoclimatic reconstructions, and interpretation of the archaeological record, many of the proposed scenarios are in direct opposition to one another (d'Errico & Sánchez Goñi, 2003). Some of these proposed scenarios will be discussed below. As noted by Ezra Zubrow (1989), an increase of only two per cent in the mortality rate of Neandertals, would lead to their extinction within one millennium. Therefore, considering the oscillatory nature of the climate during OIS-3, it is a fair assumption that climate did play a role in the demographic development in Eurasia during the Middle- to Upper Paleolithic transition. How, and to which degree it played a role in the demise of Neandertals will be discussed later in this chapter.

Examinations of cores drilled from the Greenland ice, the so-called "GRIP" and "GISP2" projects showed that the climatic conditions during the Middle- to Upper Paleolithic transition were far more oscillatory than envisioned by the original, low resolution SPECMAP time-scale (see chapter 4). The new and highly oscillatory climatic sequence provided by the Greenland ice cores led many scholars to propose scenarios including climatic condition to the demise of Neandertals.

Opposing hypotheses
Leroyer and Leroi-Gourhan (1983 in: d'Errico & Sánchez Goñi, 2003[2]) proposed that a temperate phase, which they called the Hengelo-Les Cottés interstadial, allowed H. sapiens to colonise the south of France and the Cantabrian region. During the subsequent cold phase Neandertals would have coexisted with H. sapiens in these areas, represented by the putative interstratifications of the Châtelperronian and Aurignacian at sites like Roc de Combe and Le Piage. By the end of this cold period, they proposed that the Neandertals gradually retreated to the north and eventually became extinct before the onset of a following warm phase (Leroyer & Leroi-Gourhan, 1983).

---

[2] The original paper is not available to me.

Paul Mellars also proposes a similar scenario to that of Leroyer and Leroi-Gourhan. He argues that the relatively mild climate seen between ca. 50-30 ka BP, leading to shift from periglacial tundra or steppe to temperate woodland in many parts of Europe, set the stage for the initial spread of H. sapiens across the continent. The new environmental conditions of temperate woodland would favour H. sapiens, which he describes as "ecologically adapted – both biologically and culturally – to the temperate environments of the east Mediterranean zone" (Mellars, 1992:232). This allowed them to expand along the north Mediterranean zone, from the Balkans to northern Spain. Accordingly, these ecological shifts would have the opposite effect on the Neandertals, which he describes as adapted both physically and culturally to a colder climate, resulting in significant shifts in the geographical ranges of individual groups or even a general pattern of population decline, thus leaving these areas open for H. sapiens occupation. Mellars argue that as a result of the H. sapiens being more technologically and behaviourally complex than their Neandertal contemporaries, they would have a major competitive advantage during the climatic deterioration at 33-34 ka BP, which he entitles "Heinrich event 4" (Mellars, 1998:502).

The appearance of the transitional industries has been interpreted by some scholars as the result of Neandertal adaptation to local temperate environments. Djindjian (1993, in: d'Errico & Sánchez Goñi, 2003[3]), places the "Würm" interstadial at 43- 34 ka BP. After this period, the cold adapted H. sapiens (Aurignacian seen as predominantly cold adapted) would replace Neandertals living north of the 50° parallel. Meanwhile, the Neandertals living in southern areas (producing the Châtelperronian, Uluzzian and Bohunician) would persist during the following cold phase, although gradually retreating southwards (Djindjian, 1993 in: d'Errico & Sánchez Goñi, 2003[2]). Gioia (1990, in: d'Errico & Sánchez Goñi 2003), interprets the Uluzzian in Italy, gradually occurring southwards, as the Châtelperronian producing Neandertals in southwestern France being pushed into the Italian Peninsula by intruding H. sapiens.

Some authors strongly advocate that the entire question of Neandertal extinction may be solved by climatic and environmental issues (Finlayson & Giles Pacheco, 2000, Finlayson,

---

[3] The original paper is not available to me.

2004). This explanatory model is based on three main observations regarding the distribution of Neandertal occupations during different climatic conditions:

> "(1) (Neandertals) only occupied areas of the central and western European Plain during milder events; (2) they never colonised the steppes of eastern Europe; (3) They were restricted to the Mediterranean peninsulas (and Crimea and the Caucasus) during the colder episodes." (Finlayson, 2004:149).

According to Finlayson, Neandertals were a mid-latitude adaptive species only successfully inhabiting the central and western European Plain during warm events. As a consequence of their adaptation, the relatively severe, but oscillatory nature of the OIS-3 climate brought the Neandertals into southern refugia. The climatic conditions were relatively stable during most of OIS-3 in southern areas (but see d'Errico & Sánchez Goñi, 2003), allowing for prolonged Neandertal survival as is evident in the empirical record. During previous cold events, like OIS-4, Neandertals managed to subsequently spread out of their southern refugia. However, coinciding with the onset of OIS-2, the environmental conditions in southern Iberia severely deteriorated, replacing the open wooded savanna with "denser and less-productive forest" (Finlayson & Giles Pacheco, 2000:148). These vegetational changes resulted in a "significant reduction of biomass which was only partly compensated by the arrival of high latitude marine mammals and birds" (Finlayson et al, 2001:120). According to Finlayson and Giles Pacheco (2000) this may have been the final strike against the late surviving Neandertals from this area, leading to the extinction of the Neandertals prior to the H. sapiens immigration into the areas south of the Ebro Basin. Based on the available paleoclimatic record, Finlayson concludes that Neandertals and H. sapiens populations did not reach maximum carrying capacity in the regions where they interacted. Therefore, the putative interaction between these two groups was not of a competitive nature (Finlayson, 2004). This conclusion is supported by quantitative analysis of faunal remains showing that there were substantial differences in the Neandertal and H. sapiens subsistence. According to Stewart (2004), these differences may indicate that Neandertal and H. sapiens dietary range did not overlap enough to create a competitive situation strong enough to lead to the extinction of Neandertals.

However, as discussed earlier in this book (chapter 6), the rejection of a competitive situation based on ecological factors alone is arguably too simplistic. First, one can not expect all hominid groups to constantly behave "ecologically rational". Although exploitation of the same ecological niche would make competition more likely, the absence of such a situation does not preclude the possibility of competition on different grounds (d'Errico & Sánchez Goñi, 2004). Furthermore, the term "competition" does not necessarily refer to "inter-specific competition". Competition between different Neandertal "ethnic groups" could also result in a substantial decrease in population numbers. It can also be hypothesised (although inevitably speculative) that if Neandertals and migrating H. sapiens were physically and culturally very distinct from each other, this can in itself be regarded as a possible source for competition.

The late survival of Neandertals south of the Ebro Basin has been explained by some scholars as due to environmental conditions in this area postponing H. sapiens migration. João Zilhão has dubbed this environmental and demographic border the "Ebro Frontier" (Zilhão, 2000). The late surviving Neandertals in southern Iberia produced a Mousterian tool-kit long after both Neandertals and H. sapiens developed Upper Paleolithic technology elsewhere. The rather mild climatic conditions following Heinrich Event 4 would provide relatively benign conditions south of the Ebro Basin, conditioning prolonged "less stressed, non-ritualised, "Middle Palaeolithic" life ways" (Zilhão, 2000:119). At the onset of OIS-2, a cold period following the GIS-7 temperate episode identified in the GISP2 ice core, human populations living north of the Ebro Basin would be compressed southwards (Zilhão, 2006d). As they migrated southwards, following the environmental conditions to which they were adapted, this would leave the H. sapiens with a major adaptive advantage relative to the Mousterian producing Neandertals in southern refugia. The "Ebro Frontier" model is also functional as a theory explaining the cultural development north of the Ebro Basin. If the prolonged Mousterian sequences south of the Ebro Basin were due to the benign environmental conditions in these areas, the transition to Upper Paleolithic assemblages, both in H. sapiens and Neandertal populations might be conditioned by equally harsh conditions north of the Ebro Basin (Zilhão, 2000).

A slightly different scenario has been suggested by d'Errico and Sánchez Goñi (2003). Similar to Zilhão, they recognize the importance of the Ebro Basin as a biocultural divide. However, a somewhat different paleoclimatic framework is applied. Based on the pollen rich deep see cores discussed in chapter 4, they propose a much more abrupt change in environmental conditions in the Mediterranean region during OIS-3. Furthermore, the results from the marine cores suggest that during the cold phases, northern parts of the Iberian Peninsula were able to support a substantially higher biomass than the southern parts (d'Errico & Sánchez Goñi, 2003). This leads d'Errico & Sánchez Goñi to suggest that Aurignacians were unable to cope with the harsh environment characterizing southern Iberia during Heinrich Event 4, allowing a late survival of locally adapted Neandertals in southern refugia. Towards the end of Heinrich Event 4, the benign conditions of northern areas would spread southwards, enabling the Aurignacians to do the same. Neandertals therefore did not become extinct due to climatic deterioration. To the contrary, the cold episode of Heinrich Event 4 prevented H. sapiens from colonizing southern Iberia, thus prolonging Neandertal survival (d'Errico & Sánchez Goñi, 2004).

Robert Bednarik (2006) has proposed yet another consequence of the climatic oscillations seen in OIS-3. According to Bednarik, the Campanian Ignimbrite (CI) eruption in Italy (discussed in chapter 4) (Fedele *et al,* 2002), subsequently followed by the Heinrich Event 4 would have large implications for the demographic situation in Europe. This catastrophic event, causing a rapid deterioration of the ecological conditions, prompted the rapid adaptive adjustments manifested in the appearance of Upper Paleolithic technology. Furthermore, Bednarik proposes that a dramatic reduction in population sizes, combined with genetic drift across neighbouring groups equally reduced in size, would accelerate the phylogenetic development within these populations. Bednarik therefore interpret the morphological changes manifested in the empirical record from this time period as an *in situ* evolution of Neandertals driven by dramatic changes in their subsistence resulting in major demographic adjustments (Bednarik, 2006).

Although the hypothesis proposed by Bednarik is very controversial, it is a fair assumption that the CI eruption would have large implications for populations living in the entire eastern Mediterranean zone. Ash layers from this eruption have been found in sediments throughout southeastern Europe, from Italy to the former Soviet Union (Fedele *et al,* 2002). The CI eruption is visible in lake sediment cores from Lago Grande di Monticchio, Italy, indicated by an ash-layer dated to ~33 ka BP (Allen *et al,* 1999), at the onset of an abrupt cooling event recorded in the Monticchio pollen diagram which corresponds to the initial stages of Heinrich Event 4 recorded in the GRIP and GISP2 records (Fedele *et al,* 2002). The environmental deterioration caused by the CI eruption may therefore explain the suggested almost complete depopulation of the southern parts of the Italian Peninsula until ca. 25 ka BP and in Greece until ca. 20 ka BP (Fig. 7.1) (Raposo, 2000). In fact, the Uluzzian consistently underlies the stratigraphic ash layer associated with the CI eruption across Italy (Zilhão, 2006b).

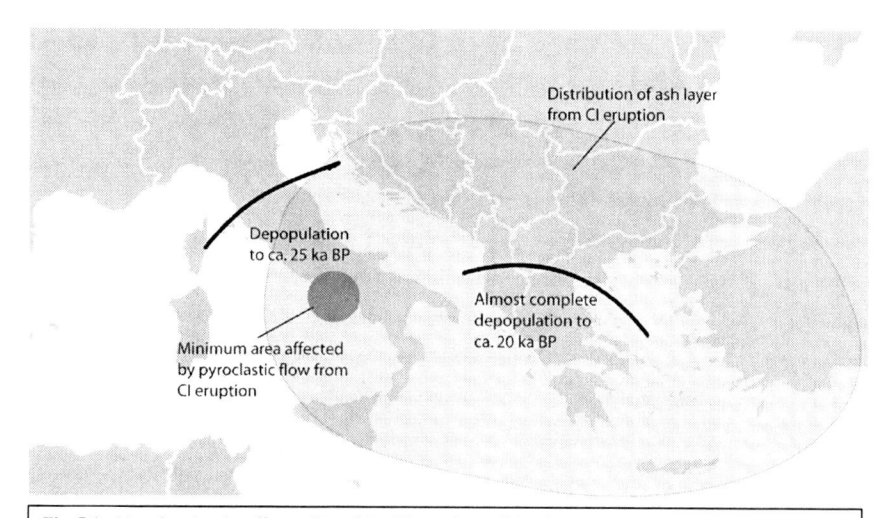

Fig. 7.1. Map showing the effect radius of the CI eruption and the demographic development subsequent to this event (after: Fedele *et al*, 2002, Raposo, 2000).

Cold or warm adapted?

As seen above, numerous scenarios of climatic conditions resulting in the cultural and demographic changes during the Middle- to Upper Paleolithic transition have been proposed. Both Neandertals and H. sapiens have been interpreted as both warm and cold adapted. Both climatic amelioration and deteriorations has been interpreted as contributing to the demise of the Neandertals. Two factors can arguably be the reason for this:

1. The archaeological, fossil and climatic data is difficult to correlate to each other because of the current difficulties in creating secure chronological frameworks (d'Errico & Sánchez-Goñi, 2003).
2. It is difficult to assess whether Neandertals *preferred* to live in a particular environment due to their adaptive skills, or whether they were *forced* to live outside their preferred ecological zones due to a competitive situation or severe climatic fluctuations (Davies & Gollop, 2003).

Neandertals are traditionally viewed as a physically cold adapted species, due to their relatively high body mass and short extremities (Holliday, 1997). However, comparison between H. sapiens, H. erectus and Neandertal tolerance to cold conditions show that

Neandertals had only a relatively marginal physical advantage in adapting to such conditions (Aiello & Wheeler, 2003). Furthermore, examination of Mousterian site distribution shows that Neanderthals were able to inhabit the entire range of climatic zones, with a markedly higher abundance of sites in warmer, than colder parts of Europe (Davies & Gollop, 2003). This proposed preference of warm climatic conditions may also be supported by the higher number of Mousterian sites recovered from warm periods during OIS-3 relative to cold periods (van Andel *et al*, 2003). Interestingly, during the period from 44-37 ka BP, Mousterian sites appear more often in cold areas and the number of Mousterian sites in temperate zones decline (Davies & Gollop, 2003). During the period 37-27 ka BP, this pattern becomes even clearer. Mousterian sites now become more abundant in areas with winter temperatures ranging from -20°C to -4°C than in areas with more benign conditions (Davies & Gollop, 2003). This can be the result of (given that the available site distribution is representative) either having to cope with the general climate deterioration during these periods, or that Neandertals were forced into these areas due to intruding populations. However, it may also be explained by Neandertals living outside the coldest areas simply developing new technocomplexes (e.g. transitional industries). If the transitional industries, and possibly even the earliest occurrences of the Aurignacian, are accepted as being at least partially produced by Neandertals, this would substantially increase both the geographical and climatic range occupied by Neandertals towards the end of their existence.

Determining whether Neandertals were cold or warm adapted, and by extension whether or not climate conditioned their demise, raises several theoretical problems. As the empirical record continues to show, any attempts to draw general conclusions based on Neandertals being a homogeneous taxonomic entity, will inevitably become undermined by empirical data inconsistent with the proposed hypothesis. The complexity of the empirical record reveals a mosaic of diversified Neandertal hunter-gatherer groups, adapting to the cultural and ecological environment that they are subjected to. Therefore, in order to fully understand the adaptive range of Neandertals, information must be sought on a regional or even local scale, instead of operating on a generalised evolutionary scale, typifying Neandertals as predestined for extinction. Although climatic oscillations may have been the direct cause for the extinction of some Neandertal groups, the very same climatic conditions may have prolonged the survival of others.

Chapter 8
Conclusion

During the course of this book, several hypotheses regarding the demise of Neandertals have been discussed. Some of these hypotheses may be regarded as partially overlapping, while others are in direct opposition to each other. How can researchers, basing their argumentation on broadly the same empirical record, propose scenarios diametrically opposing each other? The answer to this question can at least partially be explained as follows:

1. The problems of correlating climatic oscillations from marine and ice cores with actual terrestrial environmental development (reviewed in chapter 4).
2. The general lack of diagnostic fossil remains from this period, in addition to the problems of securely dating those that are found (reviewed in chapter 5)
3. The problems of cultural affiliation of many of the archaeological layers excavated from this period. Both due to methodological and taxonomic discrepancies (reviewed in chapter 6).
4. Perhaps most importantly, the problems of combining the three empirical categories above.

The increased emphasis on the transitional industries, the fast growing empirical records from areas outside Western Europe, the recent advancement in radiocarbon dating, and an increased emphasis on theoretical discrepancies, has provided an empirical record reluctant to fit into the existing hypotheses regarding the demise of Neandertals. Although organising the empirical record of the magnitude involved in the Middle- to Upper Paleolithic transition is absolutely necessary, it should not be the end product of scientific research itself. Rather, it must be regarded as a working tool, providing general assumption (inevitably inaccurate) from which discrepancies can be identified. Nonetheless, this book will conclude with a review of what a generalised (and simplified) distribution pattern of Neandertal and H. sapiens sites, superimposed on a present day map, can tell us about the extinction of Neandertals:

Neandertal contraction during the Middle- to Upper Paleolithic transition

As seen below (Fig.8.1), during the period from 40-37.5 ka BP a Neandertal contradiction from the Russian Plain becomes evident. Although the Middle- to Upper Paleolithic transition is poorly dated in these areas (Pettitt, 1999), the significant decrease in Neandertal occupation starts well before H. sapiens occupation is evident (Soffer, 1989), albeit possible exceptions to this pattern is represented by Betovo, Russia, dated to 36.5 ka BP (Soffer, 1989), and the directly dated Neandertal infant at Mezmaiskaya, northern Caucasus to 29 ka BP (Ovchinnikov *et al*, 2000), which has recently been questioned (Skinner *et al*, 2005). The fact that Neandertal occupation were substantially reduced before H. sapiens migrated into the area, indicates that H. sapiens were not contributing to the initial Neandertal contraction from the Russian Plain (Pettitt, 1999).

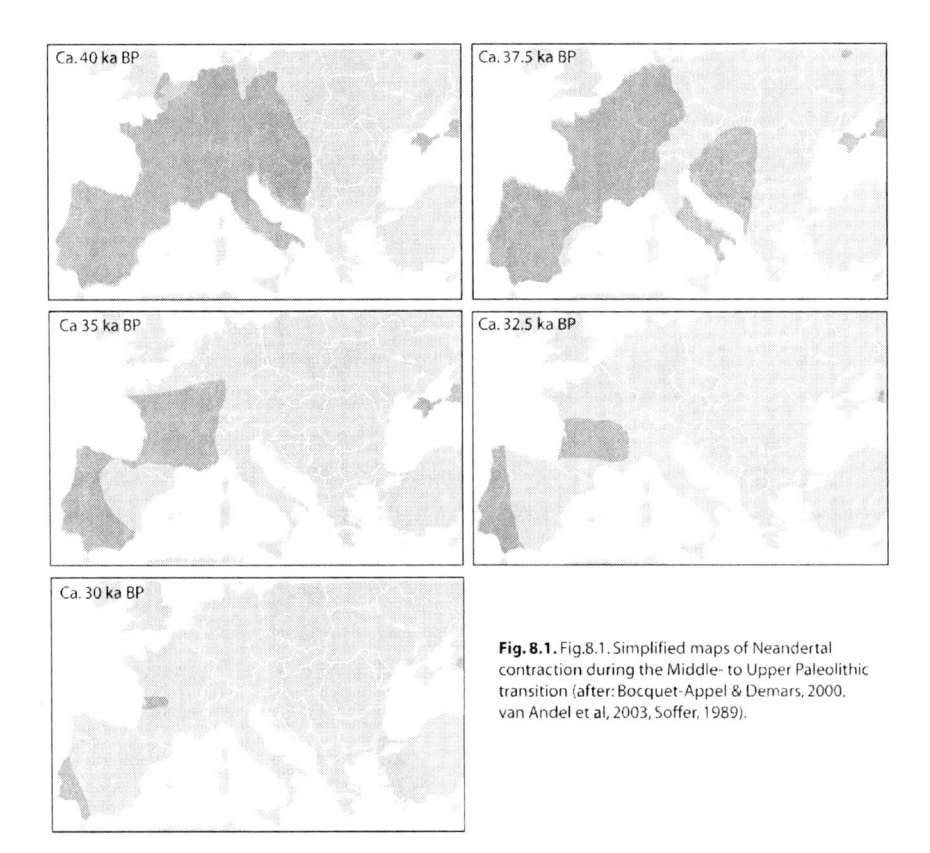

Fig. 8.1. Fig.8.1. Simplified maps of Neandertal contraction during the Middle- to Upper Paleolithic transition (after: Bocquet-Appel & Demars, 2000, van Andel et al, 2003, Soffer, 1989).

At 35 ka BP, the Neandertal occupation area is split into two areas, southwestern France and the western parts of the Iberian Peninsula (Bocquet-Appel & Demars, 2000). In the eastern Mediterranean areas a rapid population decline is evident (Raposo, 2000), perhaps due to the Campanian Ignimbrite eruption (Fig. 7.1). The gradual retreat into southern refugia seen from 35 ka BP onwards can perhaps be connected with the gradual climatic deterioration towards the Last Glacial Maximum, which began at approximately 37 ka BP (van Andel *et al*, 2003). A possible explanation for the division of the Neandertal presence zones into two areas is that they were superseded by intruding H. sapiens in intermediate areas (northern Spain) (Mellars, 1992).

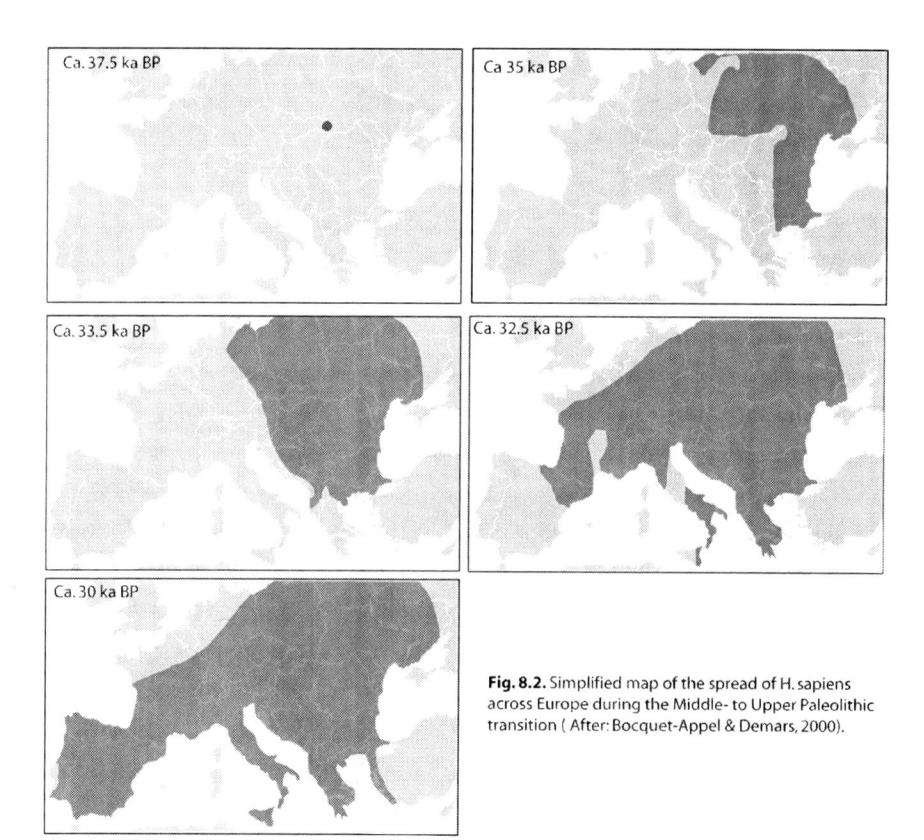

Fig. 8.2. Simplified map of the spread of H. sapiens across Europe during the Middle- to Upper Paleolithic transition (After: Bocquet-Appel & Demars, 2000).

From 32.5-30 ka BP, Neandertal occupation continues in southwestern France and the southwestern parts of the Iberian Peninsula. By 28 ka BP the demise of Neandertals is virtually complete. A few sites have provide dates that may indicate prolonged survival in the Iberian Peninsula; a questionable date of 24 ka BP obtained from Mousterian levels at Gorham's Cave, Gibraltar (Delson & Harvati, 2006, Finlayson *et al,* 2006), and the non-diagnostic Lagar Velho child burial from Portugal, dated to 24 ka BP (Duarte *et al,* 1999).

When compared with the succession of H. sapiens across Europe (Fig. 8.2), a replacement from east to west becomes evident. However, these maps are highly simplified, only portraying a rudimentary overview of the demographic development. Therefore, based on these maps, it would be virtually impossible to conclude whether Neandertals disappeared due to the immigration of H. sapiens into their territories, or whether the demise of the Neandertals set the stage for large areas of unexploited resources and thereby conditioning the spread of H. sapiens across Eurasia. A third explanation is also possible; the demographic development of Neandertals and H. sapiens were completely independent of each other, in which case ecological conditions must have been a crucial factor.

What caused the demise of the Neandertals?
As repeatedly argued in this book, Neandertals can not be view as one, homogeneous group. The implication of such a statement is that the question of Neandertal extinction can not be answered in a unilateral way. It is arguably difficult to process the empirical record down to a level of local hunter-gatherer groups, especially in regards to the large amount of time separating us from them. When studying an historical event from for example 15th century Europe, detailed information down to the level of individuals would be regarded as crucial in order to obtain an understanding of the processes studied. When dealing with societies that are as ancient as the Middle- to Upper Paleolithic transition, such high resolution information is not available. Therefore, it would be safe to presume that we will never fully understand the demise of the Neandertals. But this does not preclude the possibility for progression on this issue. It simply implies that further information must be sought on a regional scale in order to understand the diversified nature of the Middle- to Upper Paleolithic transition. Many researchers tend to emphasise similarities across regions in order to reveal the reason for the demise of Neandertals. However, the Middle- to Upper Paleolithic transition covers approximately 10,000 years across the entire Eurasian plain. Within these boundaries, numerous hunter-gatherer groups, both Neanderthal and H. sapiens, would arguably

experience a vast number of challenges; they would be subjected to a wide range of ecological and cultural contexts. In order to progress further on this issue it would therefore be productive to look at the demise of Neandertals as due to a series of unfavourable processes, occurring at different times in different areas. In doing so, less simplified generalisations will have to be made, and therefore less information will be lost in the process of formulating hypotheses.

References

Abbott, A. 2003. Anthropologists cast doubt on human DNA evidence. *Nature* **423**:468.

Ackermann, R.R. 2003. Variation in Neandertals: a response to Harvati (2003). *Journal of Human Evolution* **48**:643-646.

Ahern, J.C.M., Lee, S.-H., Hawks, J.D. 2002. The late Neanderthal supraorbital fossils from Vindija Cave, Croatia: a biased sample? *Journal of Human Evolution* **43**:419-432.

Aiello, L.C. 1993. The Fossil Evidence for Modern Human Origins in Africa: A Revised View. *American Anthropologist* **95**:73-96.

Aiello, L.C., Wheeler, P. 2003. Neandertal Thermoregulation and the Glacial Climate. In: van Andel, T.H., Davies, W. (eds.). *Neanderthals and modern humans in the European landscape during the last glaciation: archaeological results of the Stage 3 Project*. McDonald Institute for Archaeological Research, Cambridge. Pp. 147-166.

Allen, J.R.M., Brandt, U., Brauer, A., Hubberten, H.-W., Huntley, B., Keller, J., Kraml, M., Mackensen, A., Mingram, J., Negendank, J.F.W., Nowaczyk, N.R., Oberhänsli, H., Watts, W.A., Wulf, S., Zolitschka, B. 1999. Rapid environmental changes in southern Europe during the last glacial period. *Nature* **400**:740-743.

Allsworth-Jones, P. 1986. *The Szeletian and the transition from Middle to Upper Paleolithic in central Europe*. Oxford: Oxford University Press.

Allsworth-Jones, P. The archaeology of archaic and early modern *Homo sapiens*: an African perspective. *Cambridge Archaeological Journal* **3**:21-39.

Ambrose, S.H. 1998. Chronology of the Later Stone Age and food production in East Africa. *Journal of Archaeological Science* **25**:377-392.

ApSimon, A.M. 1980. The last Neanderthal in France? *Nature* **287**:271-272.

Balter, M. 2001. What-or Who-Did in the Neandertals? *Science* **293**:1980-1981.

Bard, E., Hamelin, B., Fairbanks, R.G., Zindler, A. 1990. Calibration of the ^{14}C timescale over the past 30,000 years using mass spectrometric U-Th ages from Barbados corals. *Nature* **345**:405-410.

Barron, E., Pollard, D. 2002. High-Resolution Climate Simulations of Oxygen Isotope Stage 3 in Europe. *Quaternary Research* **58**:296-309.

Barron, E., van Andel, T.H., Pollard, D. 2003. Glacial Environments II: Reconstructing the Climate of Europe in the Last Glaciation. In: van Andel, T.H., Davies, W. (eds.). *Neanderthals and modern humans in the European landscape during the last glaciation: archaeological results of the Stage 3 Project*. McDonald Institute for Archaeological Research, Cambridge. Pp. 57-78.

Barton, R.N.E., Currant, A.P., Fernandez-Jalvo, Y., Finlayson, J.C., Goldberg, P., Macphail, R., Pettitt, P.B., Stringer, C.B. 1999. Gibraltar Neanderthals and results of recent excavations in Gorham's, Vanguard and Ibex Caves. *Antiquity* **73**:13-23.

Bar-Yosef, O. 2000. A Mediterranean Perspective on the Middle/Upper Palaeolithic Revolution. In: Stringer, C.B., Barton, R.N.E., Finlayson, J.C. (eds.). *Neanderthals on the Edge: Papers from a conference marking the 150th anniversary of the Forbe's Quarry discovery, Gibraltar.* Oxbow Books, Oxford. Pp. 9-18.

Bar-Yosef, O. 2002. The Upper Paleolithic Revolution. Annual Review of Anthropology **31**:363-393.

Beerli, P., Edwards, S.V. 2002. When Did Neanderthals and Modern Humans Diverge? *Evolutionary Anthropology* Supplement **1**: 60-63.

Behre, K.-E. 1989. Biostratigraphy of the Last Glacial Period in Europe. *Quaternary Science Review* **8**:25-44.

Behre, K.-E., van der Plicht, J. 1992. Towards an absolute chronology of the last glacial period in Europe: radiocarbon dates from Oerel, northern Germany. *Vegetation History and Archaeobotany* **1**:111-117.

Binford, L.R. 1989. Isolating the transition to cultural adaptation: an organizational approach. In: Trinkhaus, E. (ed.). *The Emergence of Modern Humans: Biocultural Adaptation in the later Pleistocene.* Cambridge University Press, Cambridge. Pp. 18-41.

Bond, G., Broecker, W., Johnsen, S., McManus, J., Labeyrie, L., Jouzel, J., and Bonani, G. 1993. Correlation between climate records from North Atlantic sediment and Greenland ice. *Nature* **365**:143-147.

Bordes, F. 1971. Physical Evolution and Technological Evolution in Man: A Parallelism. *World Archaeology* **3**:1-5.

Boucqet-Appel, J.-P., Demars, P.Y. 2000. Neanderthal contradiction and the modern human colonization of Europe. *Antiquity* **74**:544-552.

Boule, M., Vallois, H.V. 1957. *Fossil Men: A textbook of Human Palaeontology.* Thames and Hudson, London.

Brace, C.L. 1962. Refocusing on the Neanderthal Problem. *American Anthropologist* **64**:729-741.

Brace, C.L. 1963. Structural Reduction in Evolution. *The American Naturalist* **97**:39-49.

Brace, C.L. 1964. The Fate of the "Classic" Neanderthals: A Consideration of Hominid Catastrophism. *Current Anthropology* **5**:3-38.

Bräuer, G. 1984. A Craniological Approach to the Origin of Anatomically Modern *Homo sapiens* in Africa and Implications for the Appearance of Modern Europeans. In: Smith, F.H., Spencer, F. (eds). *The Origins of Modern Humans: A World Survey of the Fossil Evidence*. Alan R. Liss, Inc., New York. Pp. 327-410.

Bräuer, G. 1989. The Evolution of Modern Humans: a Comparison of the African an non-African Evidence. In: Mellars, P., Stringer, C. (eds.). *The Human Revolution: Behavioural and Biological Perspectives on the Origins of Modern Humans*. Edinburgh University Press, Edinburgh. Pp. 123-154.

Bräuer, G., Collard, M., Stringer, C. 2004. On the Reliability of Recent Tests of the Out of Africa Hypothesis for Modern Human Origins. *The Anatomical Record Part A* **279**:701-707.

Broecker, W., Bond, G., Klas, M., Clark, E., McManus, J. 1992. Origin of the northern Atlantic's Heinrich events. *Climate Dynamics* **6**:265-273.

Bronk Ramsey, C., Higham, T., Leach, P. 2004. Towards High-Precision AMS: Progress and Limitations. *Radiocarbon* **46**:17-24.

Brooks, A.S., Helgren, D.M., Cramer, J.S., Franklin, A., Hornyak, W., Keating, J.M., Klein, R.G., Rink, W.J., Schwarcz, H., Smith, J.N.L., Stewart, K., Todd, N.E., Verniers, J., Yellen, J.E. 1995. Dating and Context of Three Middle Stone Age Sites with Bone Points in the Upper Semliki Valley, Zaire. *Science* **268**:548-553.

Brose, D.S., Wolpoff, M.W. 1971. Early Upper Paleolithic Man and Late Middle Paleolithic Tools. *American Anthropologist* **73**:1156-1194.

Bryant, M.J., Hall, S.A. 1993. Archaeological palynology in the United States. A critique. *American Antiquity* **58**:277-286.

Cann, R.L., Stoneking, M., Wilson, A.C. 1987. Mitochondrial DNA and human evolution. *Nature* **325**:31-36.

Carrión, J.S. 2004. The use of two pollen records from deep sea cores to frame adaptive evolutionary change for humans: a comment on "Neanderthal extinction and the millennial scale climate variability of OIS 3" by F. d'Errico and M.F. Sánchez Goñi. *Quaternary Science Review* **23**:1217-1224.

Cayre, O., Lancelot, Y., Vincent, E. 1999. Paleoceanographic reconstructions from planktonic foraminifera of the Iberian Margin: Temperature, salinity, and Heinrich events. *Paleoceanography* **14**:384-396.

Chappell, J., Shackleton, N.J. 1986. Oxygen isotopes and sea level. *Nature* **324**:137-140.

Chase, P.G. 1986. *The Hunters of Combe Grenal: Approaches to Middle Paleolithic Subsistence in Europe*. BAR International Series **286**, Oxford.

Chase, P.G., Dibble, H.L. 1987. Middle Palaeolithic symbolism: A review of current evidence and interpretation. *Journal of Anthropological Archaeology* **6**:263-296.

Childe, V.G. 1929. *The Danube in prehistory.* Oxford University Press, Oxford.

Chiu, T.-C., Fairbanks, R.G., Mortlock, R.A., Bloom, A.L. 2005. Extending the radiocarbon calibration beyond 26,000 years before present using fossil corals. *Quaternary Science Reviews* **24**:1797-1808.

Churchill, S.E. & Smith, F.H. 2000. Makers of the Early Aurignacian of Europe. *Yearbook of Physical Anthropology* **43**:61-115.

Conard, N., Grootes, P.M., Smith, F.H. 2004. Unexpectedly recent dates for human remains from Vogelherd. *Nature* **430**:198-201.

Coon, C.S. 1939. *The Races of Europe.* Macmillan, New York.

Coon, C.S. 1955. *The History of Man.* Lowe & Brydone Ltd, London.

Coon, C.S. 1962. *The Origin of Races.* Alfred A. Knopf, New York.

Cooper, A., Drummond, A.J., Willerslev, E. 2004. Ancient DNA: Would the Real Neandertal Please Stand up? *Current Biology* **14**:R431-R433.

Cooper, A., Poinar, H.N. 2000. Ancient DNA; Do It Right or Not at All. *Science* **289**:1139.

Currat, M., Excoffier, L. 2004. Modern Humans Did Not Admix with Neanderthals during Their Range Expansion into Europe. *PLoS Biology* **2**:2264-2274.

Curtis, G.H. 1975. Improvements in Potassium-Argon Dating: 1962-1975. *World Archaeology* **7**:198-209.

Dansgaard, W., Johnsen, S.J., Clausen, H.B., Dahl-Jensen, D., Gunderstrup, N.S., Hammer, C.U., Hvidberg, C.S., Steffensen, J.P., Sveinbjörnsdottir, A.E., Jouzel, J. & Bond, G. 1993. Evidence for general instability of past climate from a 250-kyr ice-core record. *Nature* **364**:218-220.

Davies, W., Gollop, P. 2003. The Human Presence in Europe during the Last Glacial Period II: Climate Tolerance and Climate Preferences of Mid- and Late Glacial Hominids. In: van Andel, T.H., Davies, W. (eds.). *Neanderthals and modern humans in the European landscape during the last glaciation: archaeological results of the Stage 3 Project.* McDonald Institute for Archaeological Research, Cambridge. Pp. 131-146.

Davies, W., Steward, J., Van Andel, T.H. 2000. Neandertal Landscapes- A Preview. In: Stringer, C.B., Barton, R.N.E., Finlayson, C. (eds). *Neanderthals on the Edge.* Oxford Books, Oxford. Pp. 1-8.

Dawson, J.E., Trinkaus, E. 1997. Vertebral Osteoarthritis of the La Chapelle-aux-Saints 1 Neanderthal. *Journal of Archaeological Science* **24**:1015-1021.

Deacon, H.J. 1998. Modern human emergence: an African archaeological perspective. In: *Dual Congress proceedings, Colloquium 17, The archaeology of modern human origins.* Sun City, South Africa.

Deacon, H.J. 2001. Modern human emergence: An African archaeological perspective. In: Tobias, P.V., Rath, M.A., Maggi-Cecchi, J., Doyle, G.A. (eds.). *Humanity from African naissance to coming millennia: Colloquia in human biology and palaeoanthropology.* University of Florence Press, Florence. Pp. 217-226.

Deacon, H.J & Wurz, S. 2001. Middle Pleistocene populations and the emergence of modern human behaviour. *Human Roots: Africa and Asia in the Middle Pleistocene.* Edited by Barham L. & Robson-Brown K. Bristol: Western Academic and Specialist Press

Deacon, H.J & Wurz, S. 2002. Howiesons Poort and implications for behavior. Unpublished report.

Delson, E., Harvati, K. 2006. Return of the last Neanderthal. *Nature* **443**:762-763.

Djidjian, F. 1993. Les origins du peuplement Aurignacien en Europe. In: Banesz, L., Kozlowski, J.K. (eds.). *Aurignacien en Europe et au Proche Orient. 12th International Congress of Prehistoric and Protohistoric Sciences.* Bratislava. Pp. 136-154.

Duarte, C., Maurício, J., Pettitt, P.B., Souto, P., Trinkhaus, E., van der Plicht, H., Zilhão, J. 1999. The early Upper Paleolithic human skeleton from the Abrigo do Lagar Velho (Portugal) and modern human emergence in Iberia. *Proceedings of the National Academy of Sciences of the United States of America* **96**:7604-7609.

Emiliani, C. 1955. Pleistocene temperatures. *Journal of Geology* **63**:538-578.

d'Errico, F. 2003. The Invisible Frontier. A Multible Species Model for the Origins of Behavioural Modernity. *Evolutionary Anthropology* 12:1-15.

d'Errico, F., Sánchez Goñi, M.F. 2003. Neanderthal extinction and the millennial scale climatic variability of OIS 3. *Quaternary Science Reviews* **22**:769-788.

d'Errico, F., Sánchez Goñi, M.F. 2004. A Garden of Eden for the Gibraltar Neanderthals? A reply to Finlayson et al. *Quaternary Science Review* **23**:1205-1216.

d'Errico, F., Nowell, A. 2000. A New Look at the Berekhat Ram Figurine: Implications for the Origins of Symbolism. *Cambridge Archaeological Journal* **10**:123-167.

d'Errico, F., Zilhâo, J., Julien, M., Baffier, J., Pelegrin., J. 1998. Neanderthal Acculturation in Western Europe?: A Critical Review of the Evidence and Its Interpretations. *Current Anthropology* **39**:S1-S44.

Fairbanks, R.G., Mortlock, R.A., Chiu, T.-C., Cao, L., Kaplan, A., Guilderson, T.P., Fairbanks, T.W., Bloom, A.L., Grootes, P.M., Nadeau, M.-J. 2005. Radiocarbon calibration curve spanning 0 to 50,000 years BP based on paired ^{230}Th/ ^{234}U/ ^{238}U and ^{14}C dates on pristine corals. *Quaternary Science Reviews* **24**:1781-1796.

Fedele, F.G., Giaccio, B., Isaia, R., Orsi, G. 2002. Ecosystem Impact of the Campanian Ignimbrite Eruption in Late Pleistocene Europe. *Quaternary Research* **57**:420-424.

Finlayson, C. 2004. *Neanderthals and Modern Humans: An Ecological and Evolutionary Perspective*. Cambridge University Press, Cambridge.

Finlayson, C., Giles Pacheco, F. 2000. The Southern Iberia Peninsula in the Late Pleistocene: Geography, Ecology and Human Occupation. In: Stringer, C.B., Barton, R.N.E., Finlayson, J.C. 2000. (eds.). *Neanderthals on the Edge: Papers from a conference marking the 150th anniversary of the Forbe's Quarry discovery, Gibraltar.* Oxbow Books, Oxford. Pp. 139-154.

Finlayson, C., Bartin, R., Stringer, C. 2001. The Gibraltar Neanderthals and their extinction. In: Zilhao, J., Aubry, T., Faustino Carvalho, A. (eds.). *Les premiers hommes modernes de la péninsule Ibérique* **17**. Trabalhos de Arqueologia, Lisboa. Pp. 117–122.

Finlayson, C., Giles Pacheco, F., Rodríguez-Vidal, J., Fa, D.A., López, J.M.G., Péres, A.S., Finlayson, G., Allue, E., Preysler, J.B., Cáceres, I., Carrión, J.S., Jalvo, Y.F., Gleed-Owen, C.P., Espejo, F.J.J., Lópes, P., López Sáez, J.A., Cantal, J.A.R., Marco, A.S., Guzman, F.G, Brown, C., Fuentes, N., Valarino, C.A, Villapando, A., Stringer, C.B., Ruiz, F.M., Sakamoto, T. 2006. Late survival of the Neanderthals at the southernmost extreme of Europe. *Nature* **443**:850-853.

Fleagle, J., Assefa, Z., Brown, J., Feibel, C., McDougall, I., Shea, J. 2003. The Omo 1 partial skeleton from the Kibish formation. *American Journal of Physical Anthropology Supplement* **36**:95.

Foley, R. & Lahr, M.M. 1997. Mode 3 Technologies and the Evolution of Modern Humans. *Cambridge Archaeological Journal* **7(1)**:3-36.

Frayer, D.W., Wolpoff, M.H., Thorne, A.G., Smith, F.H., Pope, G.G. 1993. Theories of Modern Human Origins: The Paleontological Test. *American Anthropologist* **95**:14-50.

Gambier, D. 1989. Fossil hominids from the early Upper Palaeolithic (Aurignacian) of France. In: Mellars, P., Stringer, C. (eds). *The human revolution: behavioural and biological perspectives in the origins of modern humans.* Princeton: Princeton University Press. Pp. 194-211.

Gamble, C., Davies, W., Pettitt, P., Richards, M. 2004. Climate change and evolving human diversity in Europe during the last glacial. *Philosophical Transactions of the Royal Society of London B* **359**:243-254.

Garrod, D.A.E., Bate, D.M.A. 1937. *The Stone Age of Mount Carmel: Excavations at the Wady El-Mughara.* Oxford University Press, Great Britain.

Gaudzinski, S., Roebroeks, W. 2000. Adults only. Reindeer hunting at the Middle Palaeolithic site Salzgitter Lebenstedt, Northern Germany. *Journal of Human Evolution* **38**:497-521.

Gioia, P. 1990. An aspect of the transition between middle and upper Palaeolithic in Italy. In: Farizy, C. (ed.). *Paléolithique moyen recent et Paléolithique supérieur ancien en Europe, Vol. 3.* Mémoires du Musée de Préhistoire d'Ile-de-France, Neumours. Pp. 241-262.

Golovanova, L.V., Hoffecker, J.F., Kharitonov, V.M., Romanova, G.P. 1999. Mezmaiskaya Cave: A Neanderthal Occupation in the Northern Caucasus. *Current Anthropology* **40**:77-86.

Gómez-Orellana, L., Ramil-Rego, P., Sobrino, C.M. 2007. The Würm in NW Iberia, a pollen record from Area Longa (Galicia). *Quaternary Research* **67**:438-452.

Gravina, B., Mellars, P., Bronk Ramsey, C. 2005. Radiocarbon dating of interstratified Neanderthal and early modern human occupation at the Chatelperronian type-site. *Nature* **438**:51-56.

Grayson, D.K., Delpech, F. 2002. Specialized Early Upper Palaeolithic Hunters in Southwestern France? *Journal of Archaeological Science* **29**:1439-1449.

Green, R.E., Krause, J., Ptak, S.E., Briggs, A.W., Ronan, M.T., Simons, J.F, Du, L., Egholm, M., Rothberg, J.M., Paunovic, M., Pääbo, S. 2006. Analysis of one million base pairs of Neanderthal DNA. *Nature* **444**:330-336.

GRIP Members. 1993. Climate instability during the last interglacial period recorded in the GRIP ice core. *Nature* **364**:203-207.

Grootes, P.M., Stuiver, M., White, J.W.C., Johnsen, S. and Jouzel, J. 1993. Comparison of oxygen isotope records from the GISP2 and GRIP Greenland ice cores. *Narure* **366**:552-554.

Grün, R., Stringer, C. 1991. Electron spin resonance dating and the evolution of modern humans. *Archaeometry* **33**:153-199.

Gunz, P., Harvati, K. 2007. The Neandertal "chignon": Variation, integration, and homology. *Journal of Human Evolution* **52**:262-274.

Hammond, M. 1982. The Expulsion of the Neanderthals from Human Ancestry: Marcellin Boule and the Social Context of Scientific Research. *Social Studies of Science* **12**:1-36.

Harrold, F.B. 1989. Mousterian, Châtelperronian and Early Aurignacian in Western Europe: Continuity or Discontinuity? In: Mellars, P., Stringer, C. (eds). *The Human Revolution: Behavioural and Biological Perspectives on the Origins of Modern Humans.* Edinburgh University Press, Edinburgh. Pp. 667-713.

Harrold, F.B. 2000. The Chatelperronian in Historical Context. *Journal of Anthropological Research* **56**:59-75.

Harvati, K., Frost, S.R., McNulty, K.P. 2004. Neanderthal taxonomy reconsidered: Implications of 3D primate models of intra- and interspecific differences. *Proceedings of the National Academy of Sciences of the United States of America* **101**:1147-1152.

Harvati, K., Frost, S.R., McNulty, K.P. 2005. Neanderthal variation and taxonomy-a reply to Ackermann (2005) and Ahern et al. (2005). *Journal of Human Evolution* **48**:653-660.

Heinrich, H. 1988. Origin and consequences of cyclic ice rafting in the northeast Atlantic Ocean during the past 130 000 years. *Quaternary Research* **29**:143-152.

Hemming, S.R. 2004. Heinrich events: Massive late Pleistocene detritus layers of the North Atlantic and their global climate imprint, *Reviews of Geophysics* **42**:RG1005.

Henshilwood, C.S. 2004. The origins of modern human behaviour – exploring the African evidence. In Combining the Past and the Present Archaeological Perspectives on Society. In: Oestigaard, T. Anfinset, N. Saetersdal, T. (eds.). *Proceedings from the Conference "Pre-History in a Global Perspective" held in Bergen August 31st - September 2nd 2001, in Hounor of Professor Randi Haaland`s 60 th Anniversary.* Bergen: University of Bergen. Pp. 95-106.

Henshilwood, C.S. & d'Errico, F. 2005. Being modern in the Middle Stone Age: Individuals and innovation. In: Gamble, C. & Porr, M. (eds). *The Individual Hominid in Context, Archaeological Investigations of Lower and Middle Palaeolithic landscapes, locales and artefacts.* Taylor and Francis, USA.

Henshilwood, C.S. & Marean, C.W. 2003. The origin of modern human behaviour. *Current Anthropology, vol.* **45** *(5),* 627-65

Henshilwood, C.S., Sealy, J.C. 1997. Bone artefacts from the Middle Stone Age at Blombos Cave, southern Cape, South Africa. *Current Anthropology* 38(5): 890-895.

Henshilwood, C.S., d`Errico, F., Marean, C.W., Milo, R.G., Yates, R. 2001. An early bone industry from the Middle Stone Age at Blombos Cave, South Africa: implications for the origin of modern human behaviour, symbolism and language. *Journal of Human Evolution,* 4: 631-678

Higham, T., Ramsey, C.B., Karavanić, I., Smith., F.H., Trinkhaus, E. 2006. Revised direct radiocarbon dating of the Vindija G_1 Upper Paleolithic Neandertals. *Proceedings of the National Academy of Sciences of the United States of America* **103**:553-557.

Hodder, I. 1979. Economic and social stress and material culture patterning. *American Anthropology* **44**:446-454.

Hodder, I. 1986. *Reading the Past.* Cambridge University Press, Cambridge.

Hofreiter, M., Serre, D., Poinar, H.N., Kuch, M., Pääbo, S. 2001. Ancient DNA. *Nature Reviews Genetics* **2**:353-359.

Holliday, T.W. 1997. Postcranial Evidence of Cold Adaptation in European Neandertals. *American Journal of Physical Anthropology* **104**:245-258.

Hopkin, M. 2006. Better bone dates reveal bad new for Neanderthals: Modern humans took over Europe in just 5,000 years. *Nature*

Howell, F.C. 1957. The Evolutionary Significance of Variation and Varieties of "Neanderthal" Man. *The Quarterly Review of Biology.* **32**:330-347.

Howells, W. 1960. *Mankind in the making: The story of human evolution.* Secker & Warburg, London.

Howells, W. 1976. Explaining modern man: evolutionists versus migrationists. *Journal of Human Evolution* **5**:477-496.

Hrdlička, Ales. 1926. The Peopling of the Earth. *Proceeding of the American Philosophical Society.* **65**:150-156

Hrdlička, Ales. 1927. The Neanderthal Phase of Man. *The Journal of the Royal Anthropological Institute of Great Britain and Ireland* **57**:249-274.

Hublin, J.-J. & Bailey, S.E. 2005. Revisiting the Last Neanderthals. In: Conard, N.J. (ed.). *When Neanderthals and Modern Humans Met.* Kerns Verlag, Tübingen. Pp. 105-128.

Hublin, J.-J., Barroso Ruiz, C., Medina Lara, P., Fontugne, M., Reyss, J.-L. 1995. The Mousterian Site of Zafarraya (Andalucia, Spain): Dating and Implications on the Palaeolithic Peopling Processes of Western Europe. *Comptes Rendus de l'Acadèmie des Sciences, Paris sèrie IIa* **321**:931-937.

Hublin, J.-J., Spoor, F., Braun, M., Zonneveld, F., Condemi, S. 1996. A late Neanderthal associated with Upper Palaeolithic artefacts. *Nature* **381**:224-226.

Hughen, K., Lehman, S., Southon, J., Overpech, J., Marchal, O., Herring, C., Turnbull, J. 2004. ^{14}C Activity and Global Carbon Cycle Changes over the Past 50,000 Years. *Science* **303**:202-207.

Huxley, T.H. 1863. On Some Fossil Remains of Man. In: Rhys, E. (ed.). *Huxley's Essays.* Everyman Library, 1905, pp. 111–150. J.M. Dent & Sons Ltd.

Imbrie, J., Hays, J.D., Martinson, D.G., McIntyre, A., Mix, A.C., Morley, J.J., Pisias, N.G., Prell, W.L., Shackleton, N.J. 1984. The orbital theory of Pleistocene climate: support from a revised chronology of the marine $\delta^{18}O$ record. In: Berger, A., Imbrie, J., Hays, J., Kukla, G., Saltzman, B. (eds.). *Milankovitch and Climate.* D. Reidel Publishing Company, Dordrecht. Pp. 269-306.

Johnsen, S.J., Clausen, H.B., Dansgaard, W., Fuhrer, K., Gundestrup, N., Hammer, C.U., Iversen, P., Jouzel, J., Stauffer, B., Steffensen, J.P. 1992. Irregular glacial interstadials in a new Greenland ice core. *Nature* **359**.311-313.

Keith, A. 1927. Darwin's Theory of Man's Descent as It Stands To-Day. *Science* **66**:201-208.

Kitagawa, H., Van der Plicht, J. 1998. Atmospheric Radiocarbon Calibration to 45,000 yr B.P.: Late Glacial Fluctuations and Cosmogenic Isotope Production. *Science* **279**:1187-1190.

Klaatsch, H. 1924. *Menneskets og Kulturens Opstaaen og Utvikling.* Henrik Koppels Forlag, København.

Klein, R.G. 1973. *Ice-Age Hunters of the Ukraine.* The University of Chicago Press, Chicago.

Klein, R.G. 1995. Anatomy, behaviour, and modern human origins. *Journal of World Prehistory* **9**:167-198.

Klein, R.G. 1999a. *The Human Career. Second Edition.* The University of Chicago Press, Chicago and London.

Klein, R.G. 1999b. Archaeology and the Evolution of Human Behavior. *Evolutionary Anthropology* **9**:17-36.

Klein, R.G. 2003. Wither the Neanderthals?. *Science* **299**:1525-1527.

Koumouzelis, M., Ginter, B., Kozlowski, J.K., Pawlikowski, M., Bar-Yosef, B., Albert, R.M., Litynska-Zajac, M., Stworzewicz, E., Wojtal, P., Lipecki, G., Tomek, T., Bochenski, Z.M., Pazdur, A. 2001. The early Upper Paleolithic in Greece: the excavations in Klisoura Cave. *Journal of Archaeological Science* **28**:515-539.

Kozlowski, J.K., 2004. Early Upper Paleolithic Backed Blade Industries in Central and Eastern Europe. In: Brantingham, J.P., Kuhn, S.L., Kerry, K.W. (eds.). *Early Upper Paleolithic Beyond Western Europe.* University of California Press, Ltd. London, England. Pp. 14-29.

Krantz, G.S. 1994. Resolving the Archaic-to-Modern Transition. *American Anthropologist* **96**:147-151.

Krings, M., Stone, A., Schmitz, R.W., Krainitzki, H., Stoneking, M., Pääbo, S. 1997. Neandertal DNA Sequences and the Origin of Modern Humans. *Cell* **90**:19-30.

Krings, M., Geisert, H., Schmitz, R.W., Krainitzki, H., Pääbo, S. 1999. DNA sequence of the mitochondrial hypervariable region II from the Neandertal type specimen. *Proceedings of the National Academy of Sciences of the United States of America* **96**:5581-5585.

Kuhn, S.L., Stiner, M.C., Güleç, E. 2004a. New Perspectives on the Initial Upper Paleolithic: The view from Üçağizh Cave, Turkey. In: Brantingham, J.P., Kuhn, S.L., Kerry, K.W. (eds.). *Early Upper Paleolithic Beyond Western Europe.* University of California Press, Ltd. London, England. Pp. 113-128.

Kuhn, S.L., Brantingham, P.J., Kerry, K.W. 2004b. The Early Upper Paleolithic and the Origins of Modern Human Behavior. In: Brantingham, J.P., Kuhn, S.L., Kerry, K.W. (eds.). *Early Upper Paleolithic Beyond Western Europe.* University of California Press, Ltd. London, England. Pp. 242-248.

Leakey, L.S.B. 1963. East African Fossil Hominoidea and the Classification within this Super-Family. In: Washburn, S.L. (ed.). *Classification and Human Evolution. Publications in Anthropology 37.* Viking Fund, New York. Pp. 32-49.

Lee, R.B., DeVore, I. 1968. *Man the Hunter.* Aldine Publishing Company, Chicago.

Leroyer, C., Leroi-Gourhan, A. 1983. Problèmes de chronologie le castelperronien et l'aurignacien. *Bullétin de la Société Préhistorique française* **80**:41-44.

Leroi-Gourhan, A. 1975. The Flowers Found with Shanidar IV, a Neanderthal Burial in Iraq. *Science* **190**:562-564.

Lévêque, F., Vandermeersch, B. 1980. Découverte de restes humains dans un niveau castelperronien à Saint-Césaire (Charente-Maritime). *C. R. Acad. Sci. Paris* **291**:187-189.

Lewin, R., Foley, R.A. 2004. *Principles of Human Evolution.* Blackwell Publishing, Oxford.

Marks, A.E., Monigal, K. 2004. Origins of the European Upper Paleolithic, Seen from Crimea: Simple Myth or Complex Reality?. In: Brantingham, J.P., Kuhn, S.L., Kerry, K.W. (eds.). *Early Upper Paleolithic Beyond Western Europe.* University of California Press, Ltd. London, England. Pp. 64-79.

Martinson, D.G., Pisias, N.G., Hays, J.D., Imbrie, John., Moore Jr., T.C. and Shackleton, N.J. 1987. Age Dating and the Orbital Theory of the Ice Ages: Development of a High-Resolution 0 to 300,000-year Chronostratigraphy. *Quaternary Research* **27**:1-29.

Mayr, E. 2001. *What Evolution Is.* BasicBooks, USA.

McBrearty, S. & Brooks, A.S. 2000. The revolution that wasn't: a new interpretation of the origin of modern humans. *Journal of Human Evolution* **39**, 453-563.

McCown, T.D., Keith, A. 1939. *The Stone Age of Mount Carmel: The Fossil Human Remains from the Levalloiso-Mousterian. Vol. II.* Oxford University Press, Great Britain.

Meese, D.A., Gow, A.J., Alley, R.B., Zielinski, G.A, Grootes, P.M., Ram, M., Taylor, K.C., Mayewski, P.A., Bolzan, J.F. 1997. The Greenland Ice Sheet Project 2 depht-age scale: Methods and Results. *Journal of Geophysical Research* **102**:26,411-26,423.

Meignen, L., Geneste, J.-M., Koulakovskaia, L., Sytnik, A. 2004. Koulichivka and Its Place in the Middle-Upper Paleolithic Transition in Eastern Europe. In: Brantingham, J.P., Kuhn, S.L., Kerry, K.W. (eds.). *Early Upper Paleolithic Beyond Western Europe.* University of California Press, Ltd. London, England. Pp. 50-63.

Mellars, P.A. 1973. The character of the middle-upper palaeolithic transition in south-west France. In: Renfrew, C. (ed). *The explanation of culture change: models in prehistory.* Gerald Duckworth and Co, Ltd. Liverpool. Pp. 255-267.

Mellars, P. 1989. Major issues in the origin of modern humans. *Current Anthropology* **30**:349-385.

Mellars, P. 1992. Archaeology and the Population-Dispersal Hypothesis of Modern Human Origins in Europe. *Philosophical Transactions of the Royal Society of London B* **337**:225-234.

Mellars, P. 1994. The Upper Paleolithic Revolution. *The Oxford Illustrated Prehistory of Europe.* Oxford University Press. Pp. 42-78.

Mellars, P. 1996. *The Neanderthal Legacy: an archaeological perspective from Western Europe.* Princeton University Press, Princeton, NY.

Mellars, P. 1998. The Impact of Climatic Changes on the Demography of Late Neandertal and Early Anatomically Modern Populations in Europe. In: Akazawa, T. (ed.). *Neanderthals and Modern Humans in Western Asia.* Kluwer Academic Publishers, USA. Pp. 493-507.

Mellars, P.1999. The Neanderthal Problem Continued. *Current Anthropology* **40**:341-355.

Mellars, P. 2003. Reindeer specialization in the early Upper Palaeolithic: the evidence from south west France. *Journal of Archaeological Sciences* **31**:613-617.

Mellars, P. 2004. Neanderthals and the modern human colonisation of Europe. *Nature* **432**:461-465.

Mellars, P. 2005. The Impossible Coincidence. A Single-Species Model for the Origins of Modern Behavior in Europe. *Evolutionary Anthropology* **14**:12-27.

Mellars, P. 2006a. A new radiocarbon revolution and the dispersal of modern humans in Eurasia. *Nature* **439**:931-935.

Mellars, P. 2006b. Why did modern humans disperse from Africa 60,000 years ago? A new model. *Proceeding of the National Academy of Sciences of the United States of America* **103**:9381-9386.

Mellars, P., Gravina, B., Ramsey, C.B. 2007. Confirmation of Neanderthal/modern human interstratification at the Chatelperronian type-site. *Proceeding of the National Academy of Sciences of the United States of America* **104**:3657-3662.

Meshveliani, T., Bar-Yosef, O., Belfer-Cohen, A. The Upper Paleolithic in Western Georgia. In: Brantingham, J.P., Kuhn, S.L., Kerry, K.W. (eds.). *Early Upper Paleolithic Beyond Western Europe.* University of California Press, Ltd. London, England. Pp. 129-143.

Michel, V., Bard, E., Delanghe, D., El Mansouri, M., Falgueres, C., Pettitt, P., Yokoyama, Y., Barroso Ruiz, C. 2003. Geocronologìa del Relleno de la Cueva del Boquete de Zafarraya. In: Barroso Ruiz, C. (ed.). *El Pleistoceno Superior de la Cueva del Boquete de Zafarraya*. Junta de Andalucia: Consejeria de Cultura. Pp. 113-133.

Milo, R.G. 1998. Evidence for hominid predation at Klasies River Mouth, South Africa, and its implications for the behaviour of early modern humans. *Journal of Archaeological Science* **25**:99-133.

Mithen, S. 1996. *The Prehistory of the Mind*. Thames and Hudson Ltd, London.

Morin, E., Tsanova, T., Sirakov, N., Rendu, W., Mallye, J.B., Lèvêque, F. 2005. Bone refits in stratified deposits: testing the chronological grain at Saint-Cèsaire. *Journal of Archaeological Science* **32**:1083-1098.

Mussi, M., Gioia, P., Negrino, F. 2006. Ten small sites: the diversity of the Italian Aurignacian. In: Bar-Yosef, O., Zilhão, J. (eds.). *Towards a Definition of the Aurignacian*. Trabalhos de Arqueologia 45, Lisboa, American School of Prehistoric Research/Instituto Português de Arqueologia. Pp. 189-208.

Olsen, B. 1997. *Fra ting til tekst: Teoretiske perspektiv i arkeologisk forskning*. Universitetsforlaget, Oslo.

O'Rourke, D.H., Hayes, M.G., Carlyle, S.W. 2000. Ancient DNA Studies in Physical Anthropology. *Annual Review of Anthropology* **29**:217-242.

Otte, M. 2004. The Aurignacian in Asia. In: Brantingham, J.P., Kuhn, S.L., Kerry, K.W. (eds.). *Early Upper Paleolithic Beyond Western Europe*. University of California Press, Ltd. London, England. Pp. 144-150.

Ovchinnikov, I.V., Götherström, A., Romanova, G.P., Kharitonov, V.M., Lidèn, K., Goodwin, W. 2000. Molecular analysis of Neanderthal DNA from northern Caucasus. *Nature* **404**:490-493.

Penck, A. & Brückner, E. 1909. *Die Alpen Eissenalter*. Tauchnitz, Leipzig.

Pettitt, P.B. 1999. Disappearing from the World: An Archaeological Perspective on Neanderthal Extinction. *Oxford Journal of Archaeology* **18**:217-240.

Pääbo, S., Poinar, H., Serre, D., Jeanicke-Després, V, Hebler, J., Rohland, N., Kuch, M., Krause, J., Vigilant, L., Hofreiter, M. 2004. Genetic Analyses from Ancient DNA. *Annual Review of Genetics* **38**:645-679.

Raposo, L. 2000. The Middle-Upper Palaeolithic Transition in Portugal. In: Stringer, C.B., Barton, R.N.E., Finlayson, C. (eds). *Neanderthals on the Edge: Papers from a conference marking the 150th anniversary of the Forbe's Quarry discovery, Gibraltar*. Oxbow Books, Oxford. Pp. 95-109.

Relethford, J.H. 2001. Absence of Regional Affinities of Neandertal DNA With Living Humans Does Not Reject Multiregional Evolution. *American Journal of Physical Anthropology* **115**:95-98.

Riel-Salvatore, J., Clark, G.A. 2001. Grave markers. Middle and early Upper Paleolithic burials and the use of chronotypology in contemporary Paleolithic research. *Current Anthropology* **42**:449-460.

Rougier, H., Milota, S., Rodrigo, R., Cherase, M., Sarcină, L., Moldovan, O., Zilhão, J., Constantin, S., Franciscus, R.G., Zollikofer, C.P.E., Ponce de Leòn, M., Trinkhaus, E. 2007. Peştera cu Oase 2 and the cranial morphology of early modern Europeans. *Proceedings of the National Academy of Sciences of the United States of America* **104**:1165-1170.

Russel, M.D. 1987. Bone Breakage in the Krapina Hominid Collection. *American Journal of Physical Anthropology* **72**:373-379.

Sackett, J.R. 1981. From Mortillet to Bordes: a century of French Paleolithic research. In: Daniel, D. (ed.). *Towards a History of Archaeology*. Thames and Hudson Ltd, London. Pp. 85-99.

Sánchez Goñi, M.F., Cacho, I., Turon, J.-L., Guiot, J., Sierro, F.J., Peypouquet, J.-P., Grimalt, J.O., Shackleton, N.J. 2002. Synchroneity between marine and terrestrial responses to millennial scale climatic variability during the last glacial period in the Mediterranean region. *Climate Dynamics* **19**:95-105.

Sánchez Goñi, M.F., Eynaud, F., Turon, J.L., Shackleton, N.J. 1999. High resolution palynological record off the Iberian margin: direct land-sea correlation for the Last Interglacial complex. *Earth and Planetary Science Letters* **171**:123-137.

Sánchez Goñi, M.F., Turon, J.-L., Eynaud, F., Gendreau, S. 2000. European Climatic Response to Millennial-Scale Changes in the Atmosphere-Ocean System during the Last Glacial Period. *Quaternary Research* **54**:394-403.

Sergi, S. 1948a. The Palaeanthropi in Italy: The Fossil Men of Saccopastore and Circeo. Part 1: Introduction and Description. *Man* **48**:61-64.

Sergi, S. 1948b. The Palaeanthropi in Italy: The Fossil Men of Saccopastore and Circeo. Part 2: Discussion and Interpretation. *Man* **48**:76-79.

Serre, D., Langaney, A., Chech, M., Teschler-Nicola, M., Paunovic, M., Mennecier, P., Hofreiter, M., Possnert, G., Pääbo, S. 2004. No Evidence of Neanderthal mtDNA Contribution to Early Modern Humans. *PLoS Biology* **2**:0313-0317.

Shackleton, N.J. 1967. Oxygen isotope analyses and Pleistocene temperatures re-assessed. *Nature* **215**:15-17.

Shackleton, N.J. 1977. The oxygen isotope stratigraphic record of the Late Pleistocene. *Philosophical Transactions of the Royal Society of London. Series B, Biological Sciences*. Vol. **280**, No. 972:169-182.

Shackleton, N.J. 1987. Oxygen Isotopes, ice volume, and sea level. *Quaternary Science Review* **6**:183-190.

Shackleton, N.J. and Opdyke, N.D. 1973. Oxygen Isotope and Palaeomagnetic Stratigraphy of Equatorial Pacific Core V28-238: Oxygen Isotope Temperatures and Ice Volumes on a 10^5 Year and 10^6 Year Scale. *Quaternary Research* **3**:39-55.

Singer, R. & Wymer, J. 1982. *The Middle Stone Age at Klasies River Mouth in South Africa.* Chicago: Chicago University Press.

Skinner, A.R., Blackwell, B.A.B., Martin, S., Ortega, A., Blickstein, J.I.B., Golovanova, L.V., Doronichev, V.B. 2005. ESR dating at Mezmaiskaya Cave, Russia. *Applied Radiation and Isotopes* **62**:219-224.

Smith, F.H. 1982. Upper Pleistocene Hominid Evolution in South-Central Europe: A Review of the Evidence and Analysis of Trends. *Current Anthropology* **23**:667-703.

Smith, F.H., Falsetti, A.B., Donnelly, S.M. 1989. Modern Human Origins. *Yearbook of Physical Anthropology* **32**:35-68.

Smith, F.H., Jankovic, I., Karavanic, I. 2005. The assimilation model, modern human origins in Europe, and the extinction of Neanderthals. *Quaternary International* **137**:7-19.

Smith, F.H., Trinkhaus, E., Pettitt, P.B., Karavanić, I., Paunović, M. 1999. Direct radiocarbon dates for Vindija G_1 and Velika Pećina Late Pleistocene hominid remains. *Proceedings of the National Academy of Sciences of the United States of America* **96**:12281-12286.

Soffer, O. 1989. The Middle to Upper Palaeolithic Transition on the Russian Plain. In: Mellars, P., Stringer, C. (eds.). *The Human Revolution: Behavioural and Biological Perspectives on the Origins of Modern Humans.* Edinburgh University Press, Edinburgh. Pp. 715-742.

Solecki, R.S. 1975. Shanidar IV, a Neanderthal Flower Burial in Northern Iraq. *Science* **190**:880-881.

Sollas, W.J. 1908. On the Cranial and Facial Characters of the Neanderthal Race. *Philosophical Transactions of the Royal Society of London. Series B, Containing Papers of a Biological Character* **199**:281-339.

Soressi, M. 2005. Late Mousterian lithic technology. Its implications for the pace of the emergence of behavioural modernity and the relationship between behavioural modernity and biological modernity. In: Backwell, L., d'Errico, F. (eds.). *From tools to symbols.* University of Witswatersand Press, Johannesburg. Pp. 389-417.

Speth, J.D. 2004. News flash: negative evidence convicts Neanderthals of gross mental incompetence. *World Archaeology Vol.* **36(4)**:519-526

Steward, J.R. 2004. Neanerthal-Modern Human Competition? A Comparison between the Mammals Associated with Middle and Upper Palaeolithic Industries in Europe during OIS 3. *International Journal of Osteoarchaeology* **14** 178-189.

Stiner, M.C. 1991. The Faunal Remains From Grotta Guattari: A Taphonomic Perspective. *Current Anthropology* **32**:103-117.

Stoneking, M., Cann, R.L. 1989. African Origin of Human Mitochondrial DNA. In: Mellars, P., Stringer, C. (eds.). *The Human Revolution: Behavioural and Biological Perspectives on the Origins of Modern Humans.* Edinburgh University Press, Edinburgh. Pp. 17-30.

Straus, L.G. 2005. A mosaic of change: the Middle-Upper Paleolithic transition as viewed from New Mexico and Iberia. *Quaternary International* **137**:47-67.

Stringer, C.B. 1989. The Origin of Early Modern Humans: a Comparison of the European and non-European Evidence. In: Mellars, P., Stringer, C. (eds.). *The Human Revolution: Behavioural and Biological Perspectives on the Origins of Modern Humans.* Edinburgh University Press, Edinburgh. Pp. 232-244.

Stringer, C.B. 1992a. Replacement, continuity and the origin of *Homo sapiens*. In: Bräuer, G., Smith, F.H. (eds.). *Continuity or Replacement: Controversies in Homo sapiens evolution.* A.A. Balkema Publishers, Netherlands. Pp. 9-24.

Stringer, C.B. 1992b. Neanderthal dates debated. *Nature* **356**:201.

Stringer, C.B. 2002a. Modern Human Origins: Progress and Prospects. *Philosophical Transactions: Biological Sciences* **357**:563-579.

Stringer, C.B. 2002b. New Perspectives on the Neanderthals. *Evolutionary Anthropology* Supplement **1**:58-59.

Stringer, C.B., Andrews, P. 1988. Genetic and Fossil Evidence for the Origin of Modern Humans. *Science* **239**:1263-1268.

Stringer, C.B., Bräuer, G. 1994. Methods, Misreading, and Bias. *American Anthropologist* **96**:416-424.

Stringer, C., Gamble, C. 1993. *In Search of the Neanderthals.* Thames and Hudson Ltd. New York, New York.

Stringer, C.B. & Grün, R. 1991. Time for the last Neanderthals. *Nature* **351**:701-702.

Stringer, C.B., Hublin, J.-J., Vandermeersch, B. 1984. The Origin of Anatomically Modern Humans in Western Europe. In: Smith, F.H., Spencer, F. (eds). *The Origins of Modern Humans: A World Survey of the Fossil Evidence.* Alan R. Liss, Inc., New York. Pp. 51-136.

Svoboda, J.A. 2004. Continuities, Discontinuities, and Interactions in the Upper Paleolithic Technologies. In: Brantingham, J.P., Kuhn, S.L., Kerry, K.W. (eds.). *Early Upper Paleolithic Beyond Western Europe.* University of California Press, Ltd. London, England. Pp. 30-49.

Svoboda, J.A. 2000. The depositional context of the Early Upper Paleolithic human fossils from the Koněprusy (Zlatý Kůň) and Mladeč Caves, Czech Republic. *Journal of Human Evolution* **38**:523-536.

Svoboda, J.A. 2005. The Neanderthal extinction in eastern Central Europe. *Quaternary International* **137**:69-75.

Svoboda, J., Ložek, V., Vlček, E. 1996. *Hunters between East and West.* Plenum Press, New York.

Svoboda, J.A., Simán, K. 1989. The Middle-Upper Paleolithic Transition in Southeastern Central Europe (Czechoslovakia and Hungary). *Journal of World Prehistory* **3**:283-322.

Svoboda, J.A., van der Plicht, J., Kuželka, V. 2002. Upper Palaeolithic and Mesolithic human fossils from Moravia and Bohemia (Czech Republic): some new ^{14}C dates. *Antiquity* **76**:957-962.

Tattersall, I. & Schwartz, J.H. 1999. Hominids and hybrids: The place of Neanderthals in human evolution. *Proceedings of the National Academy of Sciences of the United States of America* **96**:7117-7119.

Templeton, A.R. 1982. Genetic architectures of speciation. In: Barigozzi, C. (ed.). *Mechanisms of Speciation: proceeding from the International Meeting on Mechanisms of Speciation.* Alan R. Riss, New York. Pp. 105-121.

Terberger, T., Street, M. & Bräuer, G. 2001. New evidence for the chronology of the Aurignacian and the question of Pleniglacial settlement in western central Europe. *Archäologische Korrespondenzblatt* **31**:521–526.

Teyssandier, N., Bolus, M., Conard, N.J. 2006. The Early Aurignacian in central Europe and its place in a European perspective. In: Bar-Yosef, O., Zilhão, J. (eds.). *Towards a Definition of the Aurignacian.* Trabalhos de Arqueologia 45, Lisboa, American School of Prehistoric Research/Instituto Português de Arqueologia. Pp. 241-256.

Thieme, H. 1997. Lower Palaeolithic hunting spears from Germany. *Nature* **385**:807-810.

Trigger, B.G. 1989. *A History of Archaeological Thought.* Cambridge University Press, Cambridge.

Trinkhaus, E. 2005. Early Modern Humans. *Annual Review of Anthropology* **34**:207-30.

Trinkhaus, E. 2006. Modern Human versus Neanderthal Evolutionary Distinctiveness. *Current Anthropology* **47**:597-620.

Trinkhaus, E. & Shipman, P. 1992. *The Neanderthals: changing the image of mankind.* London: Jonathan Cape.

Trinkhaus, E., Zilhão, J. 2002. Phylogenetic implications. In: Zilhão, J., Trinkhaus, E. (eds.). *Portrait of the artist as a child: the Gravettian human skeleton from the Abrigo do Lagar Velho and its archaeological context.* Trabalhos de Arqueologia **22**. Instituto Português de Arqueologia, Lisbon. Pp. 97-518.

Trinkhaus, E., Moldovan, O., Milota, S., Bîlgăr, A., Sarcina, L., Athreya, S., Bailey, S.E., Rodrigo, R., Mircea, G., Higham, T., Ramsey, C.B., van der Plicht, J. 2003. An early modern human from the Peştera cu Oase, Romania. *Proceedings of the National Academy of Sciences of the United States of America* **100**:11231-11236.

Valladas, H., Reyss, J.L., Joron, J.L., Valladas, G., Bar-Yosef, O., Vandermeersch, B. 1988. Thermoluminescence dating of Mousterian 'Troto-Cro-Magnon' remains from Israel and the origin of modern man. *Nature* **331**:614-616.

Vallois, H.V. 1949. The Fontéchevade Fossil Men. *American Journal of Physical Antropology* **7**:339-362.

Vallois, H.V. 1954. Neanderthals and Presapiens. *The Journal of the Royal Anthropological Institute of Great Britain and Ireland* **84**:111-130.

van Andel, T.H. 2002. The Climate and Landscape of the Middle Part of the Weichselian Glaciation in Europe: The Stage 3 Project. *Quaternary Research* **57**:2-8.

van Andel, T.H. 2003. Glacial Environments I: the Weichselian Climate in Europe between the End of the OIS-5 Interglacial and the Last Glacial Maximum. In: van Andel, T.H., Davies, W. (eds.). *Neanderthals and modern humans in the European landscape during the last glaciation: archaeological results of the Stage 3 Project.* McDonald Institute for Archaeological Research, Cambridge. Pp. 9-19.

van Andel, T.H., Tzedakis, P.C. 1996. Palaeolithic Landscapes of Europe and Environs, 150,000-25,000 years ago: An Overview. *Quaternary Science Reviews* **15**:481-500.

van Andel, T.H., Davies, W., Weninger, B. 2003. The Human Presence in Europe during the Last Glacial Period I: Human Migration and the Changing Climate. In: van Andel, T.H., Davies, W. (eds.). *Neanderthals and modern humans in the European landscape during the last glaciation: archaeological results of the Stage 3 Project.* McDonald Institute for Archaeological Research, Cambridge. Pp. 31-56.

Vandermeersch, B. 1989. The Evolution of Modern Humans: A Comparison of the African and non-African Evidence. In: Mellars, P., Stringer, C. (eds.). *The Human Revolution: Behavioural and Biological Perspectives on the Origins of Modern Humans.* Edinburgh University Press, Edinburgh. Pp. 155-164.

Van der Plicht, J. 1999. Radiocarbon calibration for the Middle/Upper Palaeolithic: a comment. *Antiquity* **73**:119-123.

Vigilant, L., Stoneking, M., Harpending, H., Hawkes, K., Wilson, A.C. 1991. African Populations and the Evolution of Human Mitochondrial DNA. *Science* **253**:1503-1507.

Voelker, A.H.L., Sarnthein, M., Grootes, P.M., Erlenkeuser, H., Laj, C., Mazaud, A., Nadeau, M.-J., Schleicher, M. 1998. Correlation of Marine ^{14}C Ages from the Nordic Seas with the GISP2 Isotope Record: Implications for ^{14}C Calibration beyond 25 ka BP. *Radiocarbon* **40**:517-534.

Weaver, T.D., Roseman, C.C. 2005. Ancient DNA, Late Neandertal Survival, and Modern-Human-Neandertal Genetic Admixture. *Current Anthropology* **46**:677-684.

Weidenreich, F. 1940. Some Problems Dealing with Ancient Man. *American Anthropologist* **42**:375-383.

Weidenreich, F. 1943. The "Neanderthal Man" and the Ancestors of "Homo Sapiens". *American Anthropologist* **45**:39-48.

Weidenreich, F. 1947. The Trend of Human Evolution. *Evolution* **1**:221-236.

Weiner, J.S., Oakley, K.P. and Le Gros Clark, W.E. 1953. The solution of the Piltdown problem. *Bullitin of the British Museum of Natural History Geol* **2**:139-146.

White, T., Asfaw, B., DeGusta, D., Gilbert, H., Richards, G., Suwa, G., Howell, F. 2003. Pleistocene Homo *sapiens* from Middle Awash, Ethiopia. *Nature* **423**:742-747.

Wild, E.M., Teschler-Nicola, M., Kutschera, W., Steier, P., Trinkhaus, E., Wanek, W. 2005. Direct dating of Early Upper Palaeolithic human remains from Mladeč. *Nature* **435**:332-335.

Woillard, G.M. 1978. Grande Pile Peat Bog: A Continuous Pollen Record for the Last 140,000 Years. *Quaternary Research* **9**:1-21.

Wobst, H.M. 1974. Boundary Conditions for Paleolithic Social Systems: A Simulation Approach. *American Antiquity* **39**:147-178.

Wolpoff, M.H. 1981. Allez Neanderthal. *Nature* **289**:823-824.

Wolpoff, M.H, 1989. Multiregional Evolution: The Fossil Alternative to Eden. In: Mellars, P., Stringer, C. (eds.). *The Human Revolution: Behavioural and Biological Perspectives on the Origins of Modern Humans.* Edinburgh University Press, Edinburgh. Pp. 62-108.

Wolpoff, M.H., Frayer, D.W. 1992. Neanderthal dates debated. *Nature* **356**:200-201.

Wolpoff, M.H., Hawks, J., Frayer, D.W., Hunley, K. 2001. Modern Human Ancestry at the Peripheries: A Test of the Replacement Theory. *Science* **291**:293-297.

Wolpoff, M.H., Mannheim, B., Mann, A., Hawks, J., Caspari, R., Rosenberg, K.R., Frayer, D.W., Gill, G.W., Clark, G. 2004. Why *not* the Neanderthals? *World Archaeology* **36**:527-546.

Wolpoff, M.H., Smith, F.H., Malez, M., Radovčić, J., Rukavina, D. 1981. Upper Pleistocene Human Remains from Vindija Cave, Croatia, Yugoslavia. *American Journal of Physical Anthropology* **54**:499-545.

Wolpoff, M.H., Zhi, W.X., Thorne, A.G. 1984. Modern Homo Sapiens Origins: A General Theory of Hominid Evolution Involving the Fossil Evidence From East Asia. In: Smith, F.H., Spencer, F. (eds.). *The Origins of Modern Humans: A World Survey of the Fossil Evidence*. Alan R. Riss, Inc., New York. Pp. 411-483.

Wynn, T., Coolidge, F.L. 2004. The expert Neandertal mind. *Journal of Human Evolution* **46**:467-487.

Yellen, J.E., Brooks, A.S., Cornelissen, E., Mehlmann, M.J., Stewart, K. 1995. A Middle Stone Age worked bone industry from Katanda, Upper Semliki Valley, Zaire. *Science, vol.* 268, 553-556.

Zagwijn, W.H. 1990. Vegetation and climate during warmer intervals in the late Pleistocene of western and central Europe. *Quaternary International* **3/4**:57-67.

Zilhão, J. 2000. The Ebro Frontier: A Model for the Late Extinction of Iberian Neanderthals. In: Stringer, C.B., Barton, R.N.E., Finlayson, C. (eds). *Neanderthals on the Edge: Papers from a conference marking the 150th anniversary of the Forbe's Quarry discovery, Gibraltar*. Oxbow Books, Oxford. Pp. 111-121.

Zilhão, J. 2006a. Genes, Fossils, and Culture. An Overview of the Evidence of Neanderthal-Modern Human Interaction and Admixture. *Proceedings of the Prehistoric Society* **72**:1-20.

Zilhão, J. 2006b. Neanderthals and Moderns Mixed, and it Matters. *Evolutionary Anthropology* **15**:183-195.

Zilhão, J. 2006c. Aurignacian, Behavior, Modern. Issues of Definition in modern human origins research. In: Bar-Yosef, O., Zilhão, J. (eds.). *Towards a Definition of the Aurignacian*. Trabalhos de Arqueologia 45, Lisboa, American School of Prehistoric Research/Instituto Português de Arqueologia. Pp. 53-69.

Zilhão, J. 2006d. Chronostratigraphy of the Middle-to-Upper Paleolithic Transition in the Iberian Peninsula. *Pyrenae* **37**:7-84.

Zilhão, J. 2007. The Emergence of Ornaments and Art: An Archaeological Perspective on the Origins of "Behavioural Modernity". *Journal of Archaeological Research* **15**:1-54.

Zilhão, J. & d'Errico, F. 1999. The Chronology and Taphonomy of the Earliest Aurignacian and Its Implications for the Understanding of Neandertal Extinction. *Journal of World Prehistory* **13**:1-68.

Zilhão, J., d'Errico, F., Bordes, J.-G., Lenoble, A., Texier, J.-P., Rigaud, J.-P. 2006. Analysis of Aurignacian interstratification at the Châtelperronian-type site and implications for the behavioral modernity of Neandertals. *Proceedings of the National Academy of Sciences of the United States of America* **103**:12643-12648.

Zubrow, E. 1989. The Demographic Modelling of Neandertal Extinction. In: Mellars, P., Stringer, C. (eds.). *The Human Revolution: Behavioural and Biological Perspectives on the Origins of Modern Humans.* Edinburgh University Press, Edinburgh. Pp. 212-231.

Internet sources

Bednarik, R. 2006. http://www.chass.utoronto.ca/epc/srb/cyber/rbednarik2.pdf